LONGING TO LOVE

emoir of
desire,
relationships,
and
spiritual
transformation

TIM MULDOON

LOYOLAPRESS.
A JESUIT MINISTRY
Chicago

LOYOLA PRESS.
A JESUIT MINISTRY

3441 N. Ashland Avenue
Chicago, Illinois 60657
(800) 621-1008
www.loyolapress.com

© 2010 Timothy P. Muldoon
All rights reserved

Cover image: © *Philip and Karen Smith/Getty Images*
Author photo: Manu Punathil
Cover design by Judine O'Shea
Interior design by Joan Bledig

Library of Congress Cataloging-in-Publication Data
Muldoon, Tim.
   Longing to love : a memoir of desire, relationships, and spiritual transformation / Tim
Muldoon.
      p. cm.
   ISBN-13: 978-0-8294-2805-6
   ISBN-10: 0-8294-2805-4
   1.   Marriage—Religious aspects—Catholic Church.   2.   Love—Religious aspects—
Catholic Church.   3.   Spirituality—Catholic Church.   4.   Spiritual life—Catholic
Church.   5.   Muldoon, Tim.   6.   Adoption—Religious aspects—Catholic Church.   I. Title.
   BX2250.M785 2010
   248.8'440922—dc22

                                                                    2009039774

Printed in the United States of America.
10 11 12 13 14 15 16 Versa 10 9 8 7 6 5 4 3 2 1

Nothing is more practical than finding God, that is, than falling in love in a quite absolute, final way.

What you are in love with, what seizes your imagination, will affect everything.

It will decide what will get you out of bed in the morning,

what you will do with your evenings,

how you will spend your weekends,

what you read,

who you know,

what breaks your heart,

and what amazes you with joy and gratitude.

Fall in love, stay in love and it will decide everything.

Attributed to Pedro Arrupe, SJ

Satisfaction is a lowly
thing, how pure a thing is joy.

Marianne Moore

CONTENTS

Acknowledgments ix

An Interactive Feature xi

1   Where We Never Thought We'd Be 1

2   When We Dared to Call It Love 11

3   What It Means Not to Be Alone 39

4   How Love Opens Up a Life 53

5   When Two Life Struggles Merge into One 63

6   How Love Blooms into Fascination 73

7   When Real Life Is Lived Together 81

8   When We Had to Throw Away the Script 89

9   When We Finally Arrived at the Same Place 97

10   How Far Thirty Is from Twenty 107

11   Why We Journeyed to the Other Side of the World 125

12   How I Fell In Love Three Times 131

Questions for Couples in Love 135

About the Author 147

Acknowledgments

This is a true story, told as faithfully as I can remember. The narrative reflects both the material that I recorded in journals over the years, as well as shared memories. In all but one case the names are real. This book is dedicated to the people in my life who have taught me how to love: my beautiful wife, Sue, and our two exquisite daughters, Grace and Kate. They can claim our shared triumphs; I alone claim my failings.

But of course in any love story there are subplots that can never be told fully, and so I thank my parents, my siblings, and my extended family of in-laws. I am also grateful for the support of the editors and staff of Loyola Press, with whom I have worked on this, our second book together. Thank you, Joe Durepos, for your enthusiasm and energy in helping me think through why our story might be good to share. Thank you also to Vinita Wright, not only for your support and encouragement, but also for your clarity and precision in helping me tell this true story truthfully.

An Interactive Feature

This is one couple's love story, and it bears the uniqueness of their life together. But their journey has been marked by the same stages and challenges faced by most people who fall in love and then try to follow where that love leads.

We think that some of the key moments in the life of Tim and Sue may well have parallels in the lives of many readers. For this reason, we have created **Questions for Couples in Love** at the end of the book. Not only have we generated engaging questions from the Muldoons' story, but we have alerted you when a particular aspect of the story has a correlating question in the discussion section.

Questions located on pages 135–145

Throughout the book, when "See Question #" appears in the margin, this means that a question in the discussion section is related to this part of the story. You might choose to turn to that question right then; sometimes it helps to begin with the topic of someone else's situation before moving into an honest exploration of your own.

Or, you can go to your own discussion at a later time. Please use this feature in the way that's best for you. We encourage people to approach the questions as individuals and also as couples. May your time with these pages offer food for thought, hope for your life together, and a richer engagement with God, the author of our deepest desires.

1

Where We Never Thought We'd Be (December, 2000)

My mind is beginning to settle down, now a moderate hum echoing the sound of the engines outside our window. The euphoria of anticipating our adoption that accompanied us onto the plane hours ago has brought us to sheer exhaustion, the result of accumulated stress and hope, pain and longing. I am nodding off, then awakening, trying to find a position in the cramped seat that will allow for at least a semblance of sleep.

Sue has never looked more beautiful. Her face is peaceful, resting on a pillow against the window. I imagine that what she's dreaming is hopeful. The thought of her dreams is a consolation, knowing as I do how often over the past five years her dreams have been fraught with heartache. She was made to be a mother, yet denied the obvious route to her heart's desire. I want to touch her face, as if this physical contact might grant me passage into her dream world. Many times I have prayed for the ability to take away her pain, to enter her dreams like the angels of the Bible and assure her that God has chosen her for a different kind of happiness, a difficult yet deep and lasting happiness. More than once over our ten years together we have learned the hard wisdom of perseverance.

Eventually, I give up trying to sleep. My mind is crammed with thoughts: fragments of conversations, images of our life together, expectations for the near and distant future. We are on a plane to China. To China! How did this happen? How did I get here? In my semiconscious state I'm looking down at us, a couple who have chosen to cross boundaries of family and culture, who have already traversed a hard road and who have decided to press on toward something altogether new and therefore both exciting and frightening. I am seeing myself from a distance: still in many ways a kid being led by a woman of purpose, trying to keep up. Her certainty about this decision came long before mine, and often since the onset of her alternately forceful and gentle persuasions I have found myself facing this reality like a brick wall. Are we really adopting an orphan from China?

See
Question
1
p. 135

To slip into a comfort zone, I exercise my mind. *Meiyou guanxi:* "don't worry," I'll say to her, that ten-month-old whose blank stare at the camera has tethered my heart even before our first meeting. *"Ta shi nide mama; wo shi nide baba."* Perhaps by using these words in the tongue she's accustomed to hearing, I can make her understand what is happening when they place her in our arms. "She is your mom; I'm your dad." The scene becomes controllable when I imagine how to use the Mandarin that my Chinese-born tutor Fran has been teaching me. This language will serve as a handrail on this runaway train. I can focus on how to speak well; I can arrive as the young American professor and engage our hosts in cross-cultural dialogue; I can enjoy the trip as an exercise in social anthropology. This image is, at this moment, the only way I can even begin to wrap my brain around the situation, for in reality I'm trying to be courageous.

We are about to be new parents, which is enough to give panic to most men I know. But our daughter has been born in a different country, and we know very little about what her first months of life have been like. She was abandoned by her birth mother and has since lived in an institution with less-than-optimal attention. Over time, we will deal with race issues (what's it like to be Asian in America?), adoption issues ("Why didn't my parents want me?"), medical issues (is she lactose intolerant? malnourished? susceptible to leukemia?), education issues (will she be affected by the change in language?) and God knows what else. I can't say that I ever really desired to live a normal life, which would likely be pretty boring, but now the finality of having a mixed-race family means that the option to be perceived as normal is, well, long past. Let the stares begin.

My mind wanders back to the lessons. They have nestled in my brain, the result of the many hours I spent on the long commute to work each day, listening intently to my Walkman. "*Hen gaoxing jian dao nin*," slowly, then a pause, "I'm very pleased to meet you," double pause. "*Wo shi meiguo ren*," pause, "I am an American," and so on. Every week I read the chapter, recorded the lessons, then replayed them during the commute. The long country road to the college, without stoplights or turns, was the perfect setting for these language lessons; even now I associate certain lessons with specific places and weather conditions. I doze off, imagining a rainy day in early autumn: I'm heading east on Route 422 near Penn Run, somewhere in chapter six of the lessons, on ordering food in a restaurant...

"What are you thinking about?" asks Sue.

"Huh?" I mutter, as a crick in my neck makes me wince.

"You were saying something in Chinese," she says, perhaps a little defensively now, realizing that I was talking in my sleep. "Sorry about that."

I can't remember what I was dreaming about, but the word *yangnu*—"adopted daughter"—is on the tip of my tongue. Before we left I'd been thinking about how I would communicate to other people why these random white people would have a Chinese infant in tow. Maybe I thought that the common language would normalize the situation. I've been meeting with Fran for three months already and have thrown myself into the lessons. I am good with languages; I've studied four already and learn quickly. It's at least one dimension of this whole life change that I feel any competence in.

"It's fine. I was just imagining what I might say to people who want to know about what we're doing there." My response is one of those small signs of growth that I've recognized in recent months—I've successfully avoided the guy-speak temptation to say "Oh, nothing." I've learned that this is the answer I reach for when she's asked something I find hard to talk about. It's the shut-down-the-conversation-before-it's-begun answer, the I-find-it-difficult-to-admit-I'm-really-unnerved-by-this-whole-thing answer. I've left the door open for her to respond.

See Question 2 p. 135

"Jenny and Dave talked about the grandmas who would come up to them and try to bundle up the baby," she says, reminding me of our friends who traveled about a year ahead of us for their adoption. "They were in eighty-degree heat and humidity, and the grandmas would scold them for allowing any of the baby's skin to show." She smiles and seems completely at ease. What is she thinking about?

"What are *you* thinking about?" I say, proud of myself.

She pauses. "The gotcha moment." Another pause, looking serious. "How I'll feel when I am able to hold her for the first time."

She is a counselor. This is both a job description and a character description; she counsels, comforts, embraces, and sustains.

She understands people like no one I've ever met. To say that she is sensitive is like saying that the pope is a religious man. In the statement she's just made I hear not only a comment about a passing thought; I hear the tip of an emotional iceberg that she has been probing and analyzing both in dreams and waking moments for probably the past several hours. How will she feel? She will be able to use penetrating adjectives, rich metaphors, and insightful analogies. She has already engaged questions of what the baby has experienced, what we have been through, and how our own emotional fragility has carved out a space that the baby will enter.

She has pondered the journey that she, in her longing to be a mother, has trodden, and the work she's had to undertake at different stages to bring me, a less agile emotional traveler, along on the journey. She anticipates what we will need to do in order to care for this child and to share with her a vision of a world in which it's possible to trust, even in spite of once having been abandoned. And she has likely begun to shape mentally the choreography of those first moments after the Chinese *ayi* places the fragile child into her waiting arms. I have been practicing how to speak Chinese; she has been practicing how to speak to a Chinese baby.

"I can't wait to see your face." I say this peacefully, truthfully. It is the moment I have been waiting for these past several years, the moment of sheer happiness for her. I can imagine no greater happiness for me than to be part of that, and the realization is both consoling and startling.

Five years ago, at twenty-five, I couldn't have imagined this moment. Back then when hope was young, our expectations were fairly straightforward and our anticipation was that our life book would read according to script: college, grad school, marriage, baby. For her, the trajectory was as predictable as death and taxes. I was the careful one: "We have no money!" "Maybe I should be closer to finishing my degree." "We're both still young." Good, rational reasons, but all irrelevant; she taught me that the heart has its own reasons. She, the object of my youthful desire and the muse who stirred in my heart the movements that sometimes trump reason—she began with patience (God bless her!) to work upon me. I, the ordinary guy but also the scholar and sometimes the brooding intellectual, gradually learned to listen to the language of the heart, an insistent and passionate language that over time swayed the jury of my will. She desired motherhood, and she desired my fatherhood. Against my pro-testations, uttered lovingly yet with some anxiety, she steered me toward images of how life might unfold when our duo became a trio. Imagine the overflowing of love, she urged, when we can share what we have with someone else.

It certainly wasn't that I was afraid of having children; I was only afraid of having them *then*. I had nurtured the desire to fin-ish my PhD since my sophomore year of college, when some-thing like an epiphany happened. It was after a winter training session, when I walked back to my dorm after a workout, rid-ing an adrenaline high. I felt in my fast-moving blood a sense of being at home in my collegiate world, and I wanted to make it mine permanently. I just wanted to be a professor and teach at a university. After that day, I simply worked hard at that goal and assumed I would reach it without delay.

And so the thought of dealing with children before I had even completed coursework made me uneasy. Our early married life was, to me, miraculous; I didn't want to upset the equilibrium. The rhythms of our days, the simple regularity of physical pres-ence—a regularity we had prayed for early in our relationship, when we were separated by an ocean—these were consistent graces, rewards for our earlier periods of patience and hope. It was perhaps the very intimate knowledge we shared of each other's absence that made physical presence acute; we loved being able to look at each other every day and fall in bed together at night. My heart was already full.

But she was gently insistent. Whereas I enjoyed the garden of our young marriage, she sought the nest of a young family. Over time, the tenor of her suasion was hopeful, idealistic, even theological: *God wants us to do this.* I eventually found myself giving reticent assent, still ill at ease with the real questions of how we could afford to begin raising a family with a near-total lack of income on my part. The decision to bring children into our world was, then, about being willing to act upon trust, both in her and in the belief that God spoke to me most clearly through her. She was my sacrament. She was teaching me what it meant to love.

Ten years ago, I thought falling in love was about passion. She had walked into my life while we were students at Boston College, and I found myself simply wanting to be around her. There was no thunderbolt; it was more like the sprouting of a seed buried somewhere in the heart that I had otherwise kept quiet, in favor of being driven to succeed as a student and an athlete. I had come to Boston with the idea that it was the perfect setting in which to develop these two dimensions of my personality. To a kid from Chicago, Boston appeared cosmopolitan, elite, a launching pad to a life of intellectual rigor and cultural refinement. It was also a place where I might throw myself into training for one of the competitive rowing crews on the Charles

River. My life was about college and rowing—until, when falling in love, I discovered that I wanted more.

She was a regular presence, and over time it dawned on me that there was a reason I desired to be near her. Life was moving from prose into poetry, and heart was beginning to assert itself in front of head. By the middle of the year I thought about her constantly; I thought about kissing her, and stayed awake at night, blood boiling, wanting to speak what was erupting inside me. I wanted her desperately, and it was precisely this desperation that moved me—almost at the last minute, on her graduation day—to screw up the courage to tell her the truth of my feelings—in written verse. That there might be another side to the truth, namely hers, wasn't at that moment any part of my consideration. I was in love, but oblivious.

Four years ago, I thought staying in love was about careful, contemplative listening. By that time we began to realize that our unsuccessful efforts at pregnancy were troubling, but my pathological optimism refused to acknowledge that something might be wrong. Her suggestion at the time that it might be a good idea to pursue both medical analysis and adoption struck me as premature; I wanted to believe that things would unfold in God's good time. Yet she was again gently insistent, and my decision to embrace this plan was an act of religious obedience. I loved her and sought her happiness and could not in good conscience refuse what she saw as the responsible way to procure it, no matter how much it challenged my sensibilities. Getting some tests done, okay, no problem, but gathering information about such a radical life change as adopting a child? I was anxious, even as outwardly I showed support.

Three years ago, I thought love was about being uneasy and still committed. The tests were making it clear that pregnancy was a pipe dream, though I had not yet given up hope. She wanted to adopt a baby from China and wanted to get started. Was I ready? My answer: *no, but I will be. I will pray and I will work to be ready.* My feeling was like what I had experienced as a kid at one of the lakes outside Chicago. I was standing atop what felt like a twelve-story diving board, looking down at the water below, facing my fear and others' derision. I had seen others do this; I knew they had survived, and yet an irrational panic set in that I either had to succumb to in shame or face up to with courage. Down I went.

On this day, on this plane, being in love means that we have locked hands and set our faces toward China. The geography of this pilgrimage is both physical and spiritual, for we have moved from a place that we both know well to a place we don't know at all. It appears on our map, but we don't know yet what we'll find there. We will discover it together. Much of the earlier fear is gone, replaced in large measure by the excitement of anticipation. But what am I really feeling? Unlike her, who can distinguish multiple layers of emotion, I am painting with broad brushstrokes—I am happy or angry, worried or enthusiastic. I am still learning her language, even as I am beginning to wonder what sort of language I will need to learn as a new father.

2

WHEN WE DARED TO CALL IT LOVE (DECEMBER, 1990)

The overnight train from Rome to Paris rattles along like a metronome, producing a pleasant drowsiness. I have become accustomed to this ritual, now a routine that has emerged out of a mix of choice and necessity. I've been riding trains nearly every night for the past three weeks to save money—the Eurail Pass gives me unlimited rides for a month, and sleeping on the train means I don't need to pay for a hostel. I'm saving my money for when Sue arrives to meet me in London.

She is twenty-two and a graduate student. An adult, a woman of purpose. I am a twenty-year-old junior, part of me still marveling at the fact that she has decided to give this long-distance relationship a try. She lives in Ohio now; I live in England. I am spending the year immersing myself in a life I imagined very differently this time last year, when I was still unattached. It was only last November that I learned I'd been accepted into the Oxford program. It was a dream come true—a chance to study, to explore Europe, and to think about life as an academic.

Now, three months into the experience, this abstract desire to pursue truth has become much more personal, and so, even as I am fulfilling a dream to see the world, I miss her and can't wait to return to England to see her. I am torn between the person I imagined myself to be last year, and the person I feel myself becoming—because of her. When I arrived in Oxford in October, I was riding the high that had been growing in me over the previous year. Oxford was ritual, tradition, learning, music, and literature, but it was also the ancestral home of collegiate rowing. Nowhere could I imagine being more spiritually at home, and so it was easy to throw myself into that world. I hit the ground running, sometimes literally—around the athletic pitches and college fields to gain ever-more astonishing views of the innumerable spires that lifted my thoughts toward the heavens on a daily basis. The intensity of my mornings at the Bodleian Library was matched only by my afternoons rowing on the Isis, sometimes in a single and sometimes in an eight, training for the races in the spring. I was on fire with delight at just being there.

There was no question that it was the perfect place for me. I had first arrived on the Boston College campus thrilled to be there, and my first two years were, I thought, about as good as any college experience could be. Yet after three months in Oxford, I am aware of the sheer weight of history that settles upon this place like the mist over its towers. I studied Augustine's theology; I read John Henry Newman; I began learning Greek. But I also trained hard with a great crew at Saint John's College, learned how to fence, took long bike rides, attended plays and concerts, and mixed with my friends at Manchester College in the Junior Common Room. Everything here is suffused with tradition and the knowledge that others have been doing the same thing here, countless generations before us. I imagined the likes of C. S. Lewis and J. R. R. Tolkien over drinks at the Eagle and Child on St. Giles Street, not to mention the many other dons who dedicated their lives to scholarship and teaching in this place. I considered what life was like for the clerics that studied here centuries ago, even as I interacted with some of them at Blackfriars and St. Benet's Hall. I wondered what it might be like to choose this kind of life, one of study, writing, and teaching. There's a part of me that is attracted to this idea.

I spent many days simply drinking in the scenery. I would leave my flat in Holywell Street opposite New College (circa 1400) and walk toward Magdelen College on High Street, just to gaze up at its impressive tower. On good-weather days I would continue toward the botanical gardens or toward the river and Christ Church Meadow for a view of the spires. Often I brought my reading for the day, and of course a journal to insure that these memories would not be lost. Other days, I would bike outside of the city, toward the ruins of Godstow Nunnery and anywhere else that allowed me a glimpse of the pre-modern world. When the weather turned colder, I explored the buildings of the colleges, libraries, museums, and churches—the ubiquitous Gothic structures whose architecture at one time would have been called the latest style. There were chamber music concerts, boys' choirs, lectures on Shakespeare or quantum physics or linguistics, theatre productions, and liturgical celebrations. I fell in with the Newman Society and dined with visiting bishops. Oxford drew me in and made me one of its own. Often, tourists would wander the streets looking into the gates of the colleges, which often forbade visitors for fear of disturbing lectures or tutorials; it gave me great pleasure to see these places from the inside, often on the way to hear a distinguished scholar, and dream about perhaps becoming one myself.

And yet within a couple of weeks something remarkable happened; I discovered that I felt alone. It was not in some general sense, like homesickness. It was more an understanding that all the drive I had brought originally to Boston and then to Oxford was not enough to satisfy me. Before long, all the euphoria I had experienced left me with a pointed sense of loss at not being able to share it with Sue. I was at once happy to be studying in the Bodleian, then dejected that she couldn't be there too. I was awed at the beautiful landscape around the city of Oxford, then depressed that I couldn't bike with her to one of the historic pubs for a meal. With every high came a corresponding low, and it didn't take long for me to realize that my happiness had become very much tied up with thoughts of her.

Last year, I might have considered such thoughts a distraction. My purpose here is to learn, to grow, and to discern what sort of professional goals to set as I look ahead to senior year and graduate school. But as I contemplate where I am now compared to last year, I feel at once restless and grateful to experience regularly such a sweet distraction, these thoughts of the one I love.

With the crush of the first term over, I've had time to collect my thoughts. The past three weeks have allowed me to journal, looking backward over the past months in Oxford and the prior months in Boston, back to when Sue and I decided to risk calling it love. My travels through Europe have only confirmed what I realized in Oxford: that any sort of peak experiences, however much anticipated and hoped for, are attenuated by the absence of the one with whom I want to share the experiences.

I had imagined that the chance to explore Europe would be a series of highs, of exciting encounters in places I had read about and seen pictures of. The reality has been much more mixed. This has been an odd existence; I've never before been so constantly on the move as I have since I left Oxford. I've spent no more than two days in the same place, have traveled through different cities, different languages, different art and architecture, and even (it seems) different periods of history. Never before have I felt so itinerant, so much an outsider, so much an observer of other people's lives. And with long periods on trains to think and to write, I have become introspective, a kind of monk on the move. I encounter beauty everywhere; in the many museums, cathedrals, and town squares I've found after perusing my *Let's Go Europe*, but I encounter it alone. I am constantly reminded of the presence of her absence.

See Question 3 p. 136

When my Eurail Pass arrived in the mail a few days into the break, I couldn't wait to get moving. Within an hour I had grabbed a change of clothes and some books and was on the bus to London, already beginning to chart my plans. First, I went to Covent Garden to buy tickets to *The Nutcracker*—this will be my gift to her when she arrives. Then I was off to Victoria Station and the train to Dover, en route to the continent. I wanted to see it all. Images began spilling forth: the Mona Lisa, the cathedral of Chartres, the palace at Versailles, the Coliseum, the canals of Amsterdam, the Plaza Mayor in Madrid, and so on. Years of courses in European history, the history of art, philosophy, theology, literature—this immersion in the humanism of Jesuit schools has nurtured in me a desire to know this world firsthand. My first three months in Oxford, amidst centuries-old Gothic spires and the ghosts of English literati have whetted my appetite even more.

At some point on the evening train to Paris I realized that I had nowhere in particular to go. Interesting that in my desire to see the world I didn't consider that it was still necessary to sleep somewhere. That, and the fact that I speak very little French, was cause for concern. The dearth of spending money was also on my mind when I began to consider that this whole trip might be a big mistake. The idealism of my inner life was starting to crumble, and I was reaching for something to hold on to. What I found was the recollection of a conversation with one of my classmates—her plane ride, her random conversation with a French student, a new friend in Paris, a promise to come visit. Maybe this friend could help. After arriving in Paris I called Michelle, who gave me Céline's number.

Céline could not have been more gracious to me; we had never met, but on the basis of the friendship she had struck up with Michelle, she welcomed me to her home. Fortunately, her English was superior to my French, and so when I arrived, she asked if I'd like to go out with some friends of hers. One of them, Jean, was delighted to show off his hometown to an American, and so in the darkness of a winter night I saw Paris for the first time on the back of his motorcycle. "*Voilà—la Tour Eiffe. . . . Le Musee du Louvr. . . .l'arc de Triomphe!*" He shouted just enough each time we passed a monument so I knew where to look.

The next two days I spent touring the city on foot: the Louvre, the Cathedral of Notre Dame, the Champs-Élysées. I was initially thrilled to be seeing these sites that previously had been only images on a screen or a page. Baguette in hand, I felt free to go where I wanted and see everything. And for a time, I loved it, and fancied myself some kind of latter-day expatriate, ready to send home travel briefs. But over the course of the day, the lack of companionship began to feel wearying. With whom could I talk about these exciting places? Who would share with me thoughts about the Venus de Milo or the Mona Lisa? Or about Mass in the crypt of the Cathedral? Who would laugh with me at the sheer absurdity of seeing the members of ZZ Top in a record store on the Champs-Élysées?

I looked forward to meeting up with my friend Anne, who had been studying in Paris that semester. Before the semester had begun, we talked about getting together at some point, and so I was happy to reach her by phone and arrange the meeting the next day. It was at a café near the Latin Quarter, not far from the university. We ordered tea and caught up, talking about school and rowing. I was struck by her facility with the waitstaff—the simple activity of ordering drinks there bespoke an ease with language and custom that was still out-of-reach to me. I found myself wishing at that moment for the simple ability to connect with the people around me. Anne and I constituted a small island of English speakers in a sea of French, and at least she had a boat. When she went back to the university, I would be left alone again, mute.

That night I thanked Céline profusely and told her that I would be leaving very early to catch a train for Chartres. Ever since high school, when we studied Gothic architecture in an art history class, I've been fascinated with the cathedral there; I wanted to see it firsthand and simply feel what it was like inside, to meditate for some time in that ancient place and imagine the people who had passed under its stained glass.

I approached the still-medieval town in the early dawn. From a distance, the cathedral was visible, towering above the surrounding buildings; it was like coming upon a handwrought mountain that reached toward God. A new Tower of Babel? The view from a distance was arresting; save for the presence of automobiles and electrical wires, I could easily imagine being smack in the middle of the fourteenth century. On the train, I was a tourist, but as I approached the cathedral, I began imagining myself more as a pilgrim. I wondered what it might have been like to come on foot or on horseback.

What had brought me here? Was it simply a desire to connect a picture in an art history book with a real image I could see firsthand? Or was it a deeper desire to be in a physical space that represented sixty-five years and thousands of man-hours of laborious prayer? What was the attraction of this place for me, this place that stood in marked contrast to the Paris nightlife and tourist scene I'd left the day before?

I was alone when I entered for the first time, having come much earlier than most tourists. The morning mist lent a mysterious air to the place, which was enhanced by the relative silence of the environs. Many people were, no doubt, still enjoying their morning coffee as I made my way toward the impressive façade.

This will sound odd, but I had the urge to pray in Latin. There was something about uttering words shared by those whose liturgy had animated this sacred space centuries before, and I searched my memory for sacred texts. What I landed on—perversely—was the chant of the wandering monks in *Monty Python and the Holy Grail*: "*pie Jesu, domine, dona eis requiem*"— "merciful Lord Jesus, give them rest." But I stayed with it—it was in fact a text from the Requiem Mass, and it struck me as an apt prayer for those whose hands had constructed this place.

Eventually the familiar words of the Our Father came to mind; I had memorized them as a result of attending Latin mass at St. Aloysius Church in Oxford over the previous term. As I walked up the nave of the cathedral toward the main altar, I imagined praying with those who had come here over the centuries.

> *Pater noster, qui es in caelis,*
> *Sanctificetur nomen tuum.*

"Our father, who art in heaven, hallowed be thy name." Some forty years after the completion of this cathedral, Dante would write his *Divine Comedy* about a journey through hell, purgatory, and heaven, conversing with many sinners and saints who had gone before him, led by the "love which moves the sun and the other stars." I imagined the prayer as my own kind of communion with the saints, my way of sharing the language of these people now long dead and seeing God face to face.

Adveniat regnum tuum.
Fiat voluntas tua, sicut in caelo et in terra.

"Your kingdom come, Your will be done on earth as in heaven"— words I had prayed many times before in English, but which in this new composition of place represented something altogether new. For in conceiving of myself as a pilgrim, I began to imagine this trip less as an expression of my own wanderlust and more as a response to God's invitation. Had God told Abraham to wander into a new land? Was the father of the Israelites not a wandering Aramean, and the nation itself an itinerant group before settling in the Promised Land? And what about Jesus' own journeys, or Paul's meanderings through Asia Minor and Europe as an itinerant preacher? Perhaps my own pilgrimage by train was less a half-baked plan to see some cool sites than it was a more deeply rooted desire to understand something of the world to which God was inviting me, with Sue. I had left Oxford with little idea of what I was doing; I was merely acting upon the desire to see the world. Perhaps in some way God was authoring that desire, even now.

Panem nostrum quotidianum da nobis hodie....

"Give us this day our daily bread...." Asking God for daily bread was more than an abstract reliance on him for sustenance. I literally needed bread; my budget was about five dollars a day, and so I found myself really relying on faith to make this trip and not face anything harmful. I had no credit card, only traveler's checks, and they had to stretch for the next couple of weeks and get me back to Oxford. There was really not much choice; the college had closed the residence halls, and I had nowhere to stay.

et dimitte nobis debita nostra sicut et nos dimittimus debitoribus nostris.
Et ne nos inducas in tentationem,
sed libera nos a malo. Amen.

"And forgive us our trespasses as we forgive those who trespass against us. And lead us not into temptation, but deliver us from evil." I thought about the shysters who tried to get unwary college students at the train station into overpriced taxis or hovels for the night. At times I felt more vulnerable than I imagined a twenty-year-old guy ought to feel, but the truth was that everything was new to me. To pray in this way was offering up the obvious.

I submitted myself to the catechesis of the stained glass. There, the mother of wisdom; there, the story of the Passion; there, the story of Saint Lubin. Within these walls, my gaze was no different from that of peasants, nobles, and clerics over the centuries, and I felt small. "What are humans that you are mindful of them, mere mortals that you care for them? Yet you have made them little less than a god, crowned them with glory and honor." The words of the psalm came naturally. I stayed there in prayer for I don't know how long; standing in God's presence was enough. In fact, it was delicious. Was God hinting to me that I might be a monk?

I remembered her, though, and I recalled the feeling of her. And what I recalled, standing there in the dim light of the cathedral, was the taste of her kiss.

On the night last spring when I'd told her that I loved her, we went for a long walk around campus. We talked for hours about each other, our plans for the future, our hopes and our fears. She was heading off to graduate school in Ohio; I was off to spend my junior year abroad. She was beginning a professional life; I was continuing my undergraduate education. She had no money; I had no money. What kind of a relationship might this be? Yet we were drawn to each other. We spoke of faith and of longing for friendship, for sharing with another the deep truth about life, about suffering and pain, about the persistence of grace and the desire for someone to love, really love. Could I be that person for her? Could she be that person for me? There seemed so many obstacles in our way, so little sense to the risk that each of us wanted desperately to take. At one point all of it felt too big and impossible, and we stopped talking. None of this made any sense. And then I kissed her.

Twice before in my life I thought I had loved someone, only to learn later that I was deceiving myself and her. Twice before, kissing someone meant being infatuated with the other, excited by her, thrilled to be invited into such intimate contact. I had delighted in the kiss twice before, but had also carried with me the pain of knowing that I'd hurt her by ending the relationship. "You're breaking my heart!"—a young beauty named Laura said this plaintively four years ago, when, still in high school, I was learning what it meant to sustain a romantic friendship. But I couldn't pretend, rescind the words I'd spoken to her, that maybe we weren't really meant for each other. When she had kissed me for the first time, I thought my heart would burst. The language of her body was forthright, welcoming: "I trust you." Holding her, when only months earlier the idea of touching a girl's body was utterly foreign to me, meant crossing a boundary of both age and experience. And kissing her was an act of affirmation, a physical assent to the goodness of being desired by the one I desired.

The kiss was an awakening of a part of me that was both terrifying and fascinating. Before that kiss, sex was just something they did in the movies; now it seemed like a possibility, a choice that sooner or later I would have to make.

The understanding of sex that I'd developed growing up was based on two often competing influences. On one hand, I saw the ever-present magazines and billboards, watched the countless dumb movies, listened to the pop songs, even had a couple of friends with porn magazines. Like many around me, I learned implicitly to see sex as a commodity, one which was bought and sold around every corner of my information-saturated life. From the pages of the *Sports Illustrated* swimsuit issue to the videos on MTV, I learned the pleasure of an easily accessible hormone rush. In my early adolescence, when the thought of encountering a real girl in a relationship was still mysterious, I imagined that these virtual experiences were like a prelude to real ones, something like smelling good food and anticipating what it will taste like.

On the other hand, I inhaled the influences of my family and parish community, and later my Jesuit high school. Sex was never about just sex; it was a symptom of a much grander and more expansive dimension of what made us human, namely our ability to reach out in love to others. And when we reach out in committed love to another in marriage, ready to give of ourselves fully and ready to receive the other in her integrity—that is when sex can be an experience of mutual self-gift, of mutual appreciation. This was an extremely attractive image to me, encouraging me to imagine what it would be like to really fall in love with someone, rather than simply experience immediate sexual excitement. What if, I wondered, it was possible to really enter a relationship with someone I could love and trust, and who would love the real me in return? Wouldn't sex with that someone be more lasting than the umpteen lukewarm hormone rushes I could experience in a day?

This early positive imagination about sex in the context of love allowed me to set the boundaries that I did, long before I had the courage to do anything close to acting on my desires. The first emotion I felt toward Laura was awe, along with some desire and fear. I wanted her and was afraid of her; it nearly paralyzed me the first time we went swimming together. Eventually, awe gave way to comfort and happiness. She made me feel wonderful, and let me know that I too made her feel wonderful, loved, and adored. Knowing that I had such an effect on someone was its own form of elation. I wanted not just some random sex with her, but—in whatever way I might have been capable of—to love her, to make love with her.

I wish I could say that I came to some moral high ground, but the truth is that my immaturity and cluelessness about relationships allowed the relationship to simply drift along. Yes, we had experienced emotional rushes together, but over time these yielded to self-doubts and insecurities which, in the end, ended the relationship. When we broke up, I was dejected, pained. I had loved her, or at least I believed that I had loved her.

After that I became careful about how to love. I bided my time, wanting to be sure that if I became involved in a relationship again it wouldn't end with my hurting someone. When, as a senior, I started seeing someone again, I felt myself drawn in. She was moving quickly, perhaps too quickly for me. The progression of our physical relationship was exciting, but it troubled me. I shared my concerns with a friend—I didn't want to have sex with her so soon, because I was afraid it would entangle us. This time, I felt, it was important to move slowly.

My concerns were justified. There was chemistry between us, which for me meant that our mutual attraction operated on something more primal than the level of careful forethought. Despite my inexperience I could tell that she desired me. In my more rational moments I could enjoy the simple fact of having a girlfriend, of feeling like a man of experience and insight into the opposite sex. But when we were together, I found myself divided between the competing urges of conscience and hormones, and the latter frequently quieted the former. I wanted to be a good person, a loving person, but I also felt energized by the thrill of physical encounter with her. Where would I draw the line?

It wasn't that I lacked the desire—it would have been easy to let hormones take their course. But, although I couldn't have articulated it well at the time, I sensed that there had to be more to a relationship than sex, and if our interactions were merely repeated buildups towards sex, then there was little else upon which to build a relationship. My strong stand on this point left me emotionally exhausted, because it felt as though we were pushing the boundary I'd internalized in many years of religious education. In fact, it was because this boundary became such a constant source of tension that I began to wonder whether we were really right for each other. I couldn't have explained this to her at the time; I was just a high-school kid. In retrospect, though, I think that what I felt was that she did not understand—and didn't want to understand—why I thought the boundary was important.

The relationship didn't last much longer. In the end, I realized that there wasn't much else between us besides the physical chemistry. So we parted company.

In the wake of that experience, I'd entered college wary and dejected. I had learned that I had the power to hurt someone; I'd also learned that what I hoped for out of a relationship might not be shared by the other. Maybe I just wasn't cut out for a normal married life. I wanted to be a philosopher, to somehow rise above ordinary human experience, to search like a latter-day Plato or Thoreau for what was permanent, what was meaningful, what was beautiful in life—not to stumble clumsily from one infatuation to another, wreaking havoc along the way.

I didn't want to rush into making stupid choices. I was insecure ("Could one of these beautiful, sophisticated women be interested in me?") yet cynical ("People hook up here the way they try on different clothes"). I began to think that maybe this was God's way of persuading me just to give up the hope of meaningful sex. And yet underneath this intellectual exercise I felt the desire to love and to be loved, and it scared me. I thought there could be no one who thought about love the way I did.

Sue and I had seen each other a number of times over the year, but it wasn't until the following summer that we really met. It was on Cape Cod, where fifteen of us had pooled our money to rent a house for a week at the end of the summer. There was no TV, no work to do—but lots of conversation, games, walks along the beach, and day trips around the area. In the comfort of the large group I could learn who she was and what she thought about. It was not love at first sight, but it was certainly friendship. It was possibility.

Through our mutual friends we kept in touch over the following semester. I came to know her more and more and discovered that I enjoyed being with her. By Christmas I'd shared with a friend that I was thinking about her more often, and began imagining us as a couple. But she was a senior, and I only a sophomore, and I wasn't sure if I was being realistic. But the friendship developed during the spring, and as the leaves emerged so did my conviction that I was falling in love. I was thinking about her during the day, and I was thinking about her at night. And my anxieties about love began to thaw as I let myself imagine what it might be like to kiss her.

Standing in the cathedral, the memory of her kiss was delicious. I breathed in deeply the sacred air of this space, as if it might fan the coals of the memory and bring it to life. It was the taste that emerged in my memory, the deep fleshy taste of her lips against mine. I have heard it said that prostitutes don't kiss their clients because it is too personal, too intimate an act, and I believe it. That terrifying and exhilarating kiss stripped me of my defenses, my rationality, the façade of my persona, and all that was left was the barest reality of what was true deep within: I loved her, and she loved me. The calculating, the planning, the careful plotting of a life course that responsible college graduates do—these evaporated in the taste of that kiss.

See Question 4 p. 136

And now everything was different. Without the kiss, there would have been unrequited longing cloaked under a wet blanket of common sense. She would have carried on in her graduate studies, probably forgetting me over time and marrying a high-school teacher who brought her flowers. I would have gone to Oxford, sought out a prestigious graduate program abroad, and sought out a high-octane university teaching position.

But because of the kiss, there was no hiding what our hearts had been incubating: it was out in the open, and now our challenge was to make it work. We had to direct our thinking toward ways to make regular separation tolerable, for the sake of nurturing this budding relationship.

Over the summer she went home to Connecticut while I remained in Boston, working and training on the Charles River. Our contact was infrequent, though deeply satisfying: I would take the train down to New London to spend the weekend at her parents' home, and sometimes she would drive up to see me. Our time together was precious precisely because it was always short; we felt the shared need to write the script of our life together with each finite scene. And so there were walks along the beach under sun and moon, with long conversations about how we were thinking about the years of separation ahead. There were trips to scenic places, as if surrounding ourselves in beauty might more effectively paint them upon the canvas of a long, shared life. There were evenings at her home, when we would eat local clams or lobster, then steal away for a stroll around the neighborhood and find excuses not to go back inside. It all felt perfect.

More than once, a goodbye at the train station seemed to call for closing credits scrolling down an imaginary screen, with some audience sobbing at the conclusion. The insistence of each kiss reflected the looming anxiety of separation. I retain a physical memory of her kiss: the first, on the road after our long and fateful talk; those in the park, on the beach, in front of her home; and many others. My body recalls not only the taste of her, but also the warmth of her skin, the contour of her back, the slope of her chin. I smell her face; I relish the feel of her embrace. She awakened in me not only the hope of being lovable, but also the desire to be truthful in the way I sought to love her—to take time, to move slowly, to savor each step without a headlong rush into sex.

Like everyone I knew, I had entered college with the feeling of freedom and opportunity that distance from home provided. In the abstract, I had toyed with the possibility of casual sex, which I imagined everyone having, except me. I felt what any other typical guy felt, and there was a part of me that wanted the thrill of the chase. Theoretically, it seemed perfectly possible to hook up with any number of women, each of whom, to my constant astonishment, seemed more gorgeous than the last. Something in me resisted, though. From my very limited perspective it seemed that others were able to enjoy relatively carefree sex when both people sought only experience, not a relationship. But I rejected the idea that I could simply have sex with someone and then go about my life without any lasting consequence. In other words, casual sex seemed like a good idea in the abstract but an impossibility in the concrete. When I began thinking in the concrete: "What about her? Or her?" I began imagining what it might actually be like to be so close with someone, without caring about what she was really thinking about, or doing the next day, or wanting out of life.

I also had the sense that a random hookup might be like a rush toward a buffet table before all the guests had been seated at a banquet. It felt rude, not only because it implied impatience, but also because it meant neglecting to appreciate the rich pleasures of the moment. A lasting gift from my first relationship is the memory of one evening out at the movies, and the sensation of touching Laura's hand. I can't recall who touched whom—though something tells me it was "accidental" on both our parts. In any case, the experience was one of heightened sensation: I was attracted to her, and the rush of simply feeling her fingers on mine felt like a wave crashing on the shore. For most of the movie (God help me if I can even remember what we were watching), her hand grazed lightly over mine, and I in turn explored the contours of palm, wrist, and finger. I delighted in the soft texture of her skin (*yes*), the gentle feeling of her light and graceful touch (*yes*), the feeling of affirmation in her *yes*. It was like that for over an hour: hand in hand, sometimes squeezing, sometimes caressing, sometimes simply touching, and it was glorious. I don't think we were able to speak about it much after the movie was over, sensing that no words could really approach what we had experienced.

I guarded the memory of that sensuous contemplation and carried it with me into last spring. There were Sue's eyes, looking at mine, then looking away, at the thought that this idea of a relationship didn't make sense. Here was my own sense of foreboding, of terror, at having thrown open my heart and awaiting the consequences. There was my reason, calculating robotically. And then, from nowhere, arose a slight wind of courage, and I faced her, and allowed my face to drift into hers. When we kissed, I asked time to move more slowly, to allow me to pay attention and to savor. There is a world in each kiss, and a world in the memory of each kiss.

In the cathedral, thinking of her kiss, she was present to me again, if only for a while, in the silence.

When I left there that afternoon, I felt as if I'd undergone a kind of ordination. Any lingering thoughts of philosophical bachelorhood were long gone, replaced by the certainty that in this woman's kiss was God's word, made flesh. Inside the cathedral, my imagination roved through medieval monastic texts and florid romantic poetry. I was a pilgrim, a person of prayer, moving toward an unknown place where I might encounter the mystery of God. The pilgrims of old often heard a call to the monastery or the convent, but in the memory of her kiss and in the restless anticipation of seeing her again, I heard a call toward a domestic church, a holy hearth, a sanctified home where I would go to dwell with my beloved. The cathedral was a holy place, a place of liturgy and of private prayer, of devotion in word and art made sacred over eight centuries of worship, and it was good to be there. And yet when I departed from its dark interior, suffused as it was with brilliant flames of stained-glass filtered light, into the eye-straining brightness of the afternoon sun, I felt newly missioned.

Back in May, when she and I were still talking through what a new relationship might be like, I observed that it was preferable to live with the risk of both real joy and real suffering, rather than to live a safe, comfortable, sanitized, unremarkable life. I think about that statement frequently these days; it has become a kind of mission statement for me, especially now that sometimes highs and lows tumble awkwardly upon one another like young brothers wrestling. One moment I am breathing the fresh air over a stunningly beautiful city scene, imagining life there a hundred or a thousand years ago, and the next moment I am glancing at my watch and running full tilt back toward the train station so I can catch the one train that will provide me rest for the night. This is the itinerary I have prepared for myself; it is mine alone, and even in its stresses I feel alive. The stories I will be able to tell her when we meet in a few days!

The worst of my learning curve was behind me as I rode the train from Heidelberg to Florence, where I met my friends Derek and Tom. Traveling with them for the next several days lent stability to the journey. The pace was slower, but the experiences were rich and the conversations consoling.

The Uffizi Gallery and the Galleria dell'Accademia were first, all of us looking forward to seeing the Botticellis and Michelangelo's *David*. At the Accademia, we split up; I walked through a hallway and was amazed at the unfinished Michelangelo sculptures, each of which seemed like living beings trapped within marble.

Here there was an arm and a torso straining to lift itself out of the rock, its head locked within a boulder.

There was another, a full figure whose entire rear side was still embedded, all hope lost of being freed to stand on its own. The human condition, I thought to myself.

I became aware of my own mobility, my own musculature able to operate freely, when I entered the overwhelming chamber where there appeared the *David*. I had to sit down. The contrast was stunning. Whereas the other figures were forever tethered to the raw material, here was a figure that emerged like light from its source. I half thought that he would jump down and run away, but for his determined look, which seemed to carry him to some greater task in some unforeseen future. I stared for several minutes, then got up to walk around him and see him from different angles. "This is rock," I had to remind myself—rock, earth, clay, soil, the stuff of which mountains are made, transformed, transfigured. In my awe I hoped that the God I worshipped might have a similar power over living clay.

Saint Ignatius of Loyola once suggested that God was like a sculptor and that we are like blocks of wood in his hands. In the gallery, I confronted the question of what kind of sculpture (blockhead?) I am. Unfinished, yes—but would I remain so, or allow God to continue to shape me into something like what exploded before my eyes in this gallery? Am I working at cross-purposes, dodging the painful chiseling for fear that he is not skilled enough to bring forth beauty from the block? Perhaps more to the point, I wondered whether my desire for freedom was like the straining of the unfinished sculptures—futile and premature, like yanking a flower from the ground in order to see it in full bloom at a moment's notice. Here I was, having run around Europe gorging myself on cities and cultures as if they constituted some kind of smorgasbord, unable to simply stop and rest in any one of the moments that unfolded before me. Here I was at that moment, drinking in the deep draught of one sculpture—just one, after having seen many works of art—which forced me to stop, and pay attention. Perhaps something small, like a hazelnut or a sculpture—or a person—could open up the world to me, could allow me to turn from the willy-nilly desire to see everything to the more discreet desire to understand one thing well.

I know I am restless by nature; I know that I feel the temptation to indulge different experiences. Depth takes time; depth requires energy, attention, slowing down. And I have always felt that slowing down was like succumbing to some weakness, some character flaw. I am about energy, passion, drive; I am kinetic; I am about action, desiring, striving, seeking, never to yield. Now I wonder if I have missed something basic.

I imagine the time that Michelangelo must have spent on this work of art. So many unfinished pieces languished in the hallways outside, like discarded loves. But this one radiated like the sun in this gallery; he must have poured his heart and soul into this work. What would it be like to be passionate about one thing so powerfully? What would it be like to risk one's energies for days and weeks and months on that one something, mindful that failure was always a possibility? What might it be like to treat one's beloved in that way, pouring heart and soul and mind and strength into perfecting that one relationship, making it daily into a thing of incredible beauty, a pearl of great price, yet still at such great risk?

Perhaps God sees me this way, I thought. *What kind of sculpture am I?* Or better, *What kind of sculpture are we, the two of us emerging slowly as a single work of art, like Rodin's lovers?* Once upon a time I had thought of myself as a single individual whose life story would unfold amidst the comings and goings of a varied supporting cast. But as this year progressed, it was becoming clearer that mine was only one part of a larger story, one that involved her and who knows who else.

In the poem I had written her last spring, I made reference to John Keats's "Ode on a Grecian Urn." The image of the pursuing lover frozen forever in the picture on the urn, never able to reach his beloved—this was what I feared would be my fate. But today the story is different. I am no character on the urn; I have kissed her and tasted how "beauty is truth, and truth beauty." Neither am I a David, focused resolutely on a single task, called by God to defeat an enemy with five smooth stones. I am still a pilgrim, and I do not know where God is leading me, or what kind of person he is creating me to be.

The image of the *David* stays with me, even after what remains in my memory as a lovely day around Florence—the Duomo, the monastery of San Miniato, watching the scullers on the Arno, listening to the organ concert in an out-of-the-way church. Derek, Tom, and I had a great time wandering around, and I really appreciated having friends to talk with along the way. The wandering was still the same, but the companionship made all the difference. I had learned in my previous semester in Latin that the root of the word *companion* is "breaking bread together," and the image struck me as incredibly apt under these circumstances. I did the same walking around,, and consumed the same bread and water, but the memory of the experience is much richer.

Over the next couple of days, we traveled from Florence to Venice and ultimately to Rome, where we were looking forward to spending Christmas Eve. I wanted to go to the Midnight Mass at the Vatican, as well as see the Coliseum, Palatine Hill, and other sites of classical antiquity. My first year at Boston College was an immersion in classical literature, and I had read the likes of Virgil and Cicero enough to want to see some of its history firsthand. I came to Rome energized by the previous few days. So it was with lifted spirits that I saw the Eternal City for the first time, and fell in love with it. I just loved being there, even before seeing anything beyond the ordinary streets. I delighted in looking at manhole covers, stamped as they were with the ancient "SPQR"—*Senatus Populusque Romanus* or "the Roman Senate and People"—which was once emblazoned on the banners of the ancient Republic. I loved hearing myself try to speak Italian (how hard could it be, I thought, if I already know Latin?) using the phrasebook that I'd bought for the occasion. I could live here, I thought, wondering if perhaps it might not be out of the question to return one day as a graduate student in theology.

Our first visit was to the Vatican, knowing that with Christmas coming the next day it would be wise to get there early and see Saint Peter's Basilica. The Sistine Chapel was already closed for the holiday, as was the Vatican Library. But the basilica was open, at least for the afternoon before preparations for Midnight Mass were in full throttle. Having been in several grand cathedrals already—not only in Chartres, but also London, Paris, Lyon, Cologne, and Vienna—I was not expecting Saint Peter's to be so surprisingly awe-inspiring. All the earlier cathedrals had been constructed during the High Middle Ages, but Saint Peter's was a Renaissance structure the size of an airplane hangar. Its color, its scale, its significance struck me the moment I walked in and turned to the right to see Michelangelo's *Pietà*, then looked straight ahead and up to see the immense cupola.

I wandered around, drinking in the artwork and symbolism around the basilica. I walked along the perimeter, reading the scriptural texts from the Latin Vulgate Bible: "You are Peter, and upon this rock I will build my church," and so on. (That night, when I saw a man standing atop the cupola and seeing that the letters were twice his height, I gained a greater appreciation for the size of the structure.) I gazed at Bernini's columns, which looked so familiar from pictures and videos. I took in the alabaster window of the Holy Spirit, depicted as a dove, and the many side chapels. Here were snapshots from Church history, a three-dimensional family album that unfolded over the centuries and the various iterations of the basilica itself.

After returning to the *pensione* we met up with Anne, who had traveled from Paris for the same purpose of being in Rome for Christmas. The four of us went back to the basilica early that evening, in order to wait in line for the standing-room-only space at Midnight Mass. The time passed quickly; we caught each other up on our respective travels and talked with other pilgrims who had descended on Saint Peter's Square. Fortunately, we were close enough to the front of the queue that we were able to stand fairly close to the main altar, in the corner of the left transept, with a pretty good view of where Pope John Paul II would be celebrating Mass. Not surprisingly, the space filled quickly. Surprisingly, people were rude, jockeying elbows to find the best position from which to see the altar. Perhaps it's just me, I thought, but I would have hoped that a little more generosity would prevail under these circumstances than at a Bears-Packers game.

Still, the situation was mesmerizing. Here were thousands of people from hundreds of nations—religious men and women in their respective habits; bishops, cardinals, and the pope; the Swiss Guards in their distinctive uniforms. This was pageantry like few Americans really know; seldom before did I feel so certainly that I was doing something historic. We experienced a Latin Mass; readings in English and Spanish, songs in Polish, Vietnamese, and Kiswahili; prayers in French and German and Italian. I was right in the middle of the world.

It was not a prayerful experience, as I had previously understood them—this was a mad rush of humanity, particularly at the celebration of Communion. There was no quiet, no sense of interiority, no movement of contrition or thankfulness or praise. Still, it was an experience of prayer, of drawing me outside my small world and into one much grander and more challenging. I began to wonder what sort of pilgrimages these others around me had undertaken in order to be here, especially those who had traveled thousands of miles, perhaps with little money. What drew them? Why had they come? And for that matter, why had I come? What exactly were we all after?

There were the obvious answers: a love of history and art, and those great repositories of Western culture. But museums don't attract people to events like this one. And so there emerged another, perhaps more subtle answer: a shared belief, a shared religion—a sharing that transcended national, ethnic, and economic boundaries. I was here with people from literally every part of the world, and I had never before known such diversity. I wanted to echo Socrates: the world is my home, the world which is described in Socrates' Greek as *katholikos*, universal.

True, it was not the whole world—I thought of my Jewish and Protestant friends back in Oxford and Boston, and realized that this was still an incomplete community. And in part because of that realization I looked for a yet more subtle answer to my question of why we were here, for it was unsatisfying to imagine that we thought of ourselves as comprising just an imperfect community doing its own thing, like any club or social organization. For myself—I could not speak for these sisters and brothers jammed around me—I observed that I was here out of hope, that my belief in the reality of Christ made me a part of something that could not stop short of hope for the entire human family. And so I found myself taking odd comfort in the waves of elbows and shoulders.

But the truth is that this is my church; this is the community into which I was born and which has given me a language with which I have come to understand the movements of God in history and even in my own life. And nowhere have I felt those movements more strongly than when I am with her; quite simply, when I am with her I want to be holy. I want to be able to love her perfectly, without selfishness and without the kind of limitation that stifled my earlier attempts at love. Because of her, God has a human face, and it is a face that beckons me to become better than I am right now. I don't need to engage in flights of imagination to know that God loves me: it's in her voice, her assuring, sonorous voice telling me that she loves me, when I can't really place my finger on exactly why. I guess I am in this church because it is a place where I can say thank you, ask for help, and even sometimes rage when the strain is too much. This is where I hear the voice of God, where I turn down the static of my rational mind and listen to deeper chords within me resonating with those around me. I love worshipping a God who has become one of us, whose passion for us meant willingness to sacrifice his very self. Maybe some of the people here have come just for the sake of seeing a celebrity, but I suppose that happened to Jesus too.

The Mass ended in the wee hours of the morning, and we all filed out into Saint Peter's Square. Near the giant crèche we stood in a circle, just soaking in the atmosphere, and someone started singing "Silent Night." "O Come All Ye Faithful" followed, and soon we were singing just about everything we could remember. We even had a request or two from some other pilgrims, in languages we couldn't understand. When we finally walked back to our lodging at around 4:00 a.m., we were exhilarated and exhausted. For my part, it was the culmination of my pilgrimage, or at least this phase of it. It's been three weeks of nonstop travel around Europe, but now I am on my way back to England and, after what once felt like it would be halfway to forever, a reunion with my beloved.

3

WHAT IT MEANS
NOT TO BE ALONE
(DECEMBER, 1990 TO
JANUARY, 1991)

"Wow, she must be pretty special!" Marcie looks amazed. I have just described why I will not join her and some other Oxford friends who will gather in preparation for the New Year celebration, just days away. They are on their way to York, where they are renting a house during the holiday. I have just arrived after the long trip from Rome, and tomorrow I will be on my way to Heathrow to meet Sue. We will spend a few days in Oxford and London before heading west to Dublin. I am a little pale, a lot hungry, and exhilarated; Marcie sees it in my eyes.

The trip there is partly at the suggestion of Sue's parents, whose friends have offered their home for our visit. The suggestion is perfect—I have dreamed about the place since my encounter with James Joyce's *The Dubliners* and feel it my duty as a Muldoon to see it for myself. (But on the other hand, I begin to wonder whether staying with friends of the family might be a way of their keeping tabs on us.)

My doubts dissipate when I start thinking about seeing her tomorrow. She is exquisitely Irish American, freckled and fair-skinned, with a smile that says "kiss me." At least that was the conclusion I had reached by the end of last Saint Patrick's Day, when she and I took the T to South Boston for the parade. A simple and safe idea it was, at the time; we went as friends. She, a senior, was not someone I, a lowly sophomore, imagined I could easily ask out on a date (no one dates these days, anyway), so when she mentioned that she wanted to go see the parade (aha!) I said maybe we could share the ride there, since I too was planning to go (well, I am now).

How perfect the long ride there, the long parade, the long ride back! By the end of the day there was no question in my mind that she was wonderful. Oh, those eyes! It was all I could do to prolong our time together, to extract from the day a few more precious minutes in her presence.

A couple of weeks later I seized another opportunity. This time it was an Irish mass, complete with uilleann pipes and bodhrán. She mentioned that her parents would be coming up from their home in Connecticut—would I care to join them? I donned my Donegal tweeds and headed across campus to meet them all. "Good morning to you, Mr. and Mrs. O'Farrell," I said, feeling like a character in a latter-day Joyce story. They, second-generations like my own parents, welcomed me as one of their own. At the time, they thought I was an aspiring seminarian, as I was majoring in theology. I was simply a friend of their daughter's, and one of their people. What could be more perfect?

After Mass we went to brunch. They were happy to see their oldest daughter in the middle of the semester; we all enjoyed the Mass, the chance to celebrate both faith and heritage together; I enjoyed sitting next to her in such a familiar way. The talk was about Ireland—I, sharing the story of my great-grandfather's journey from County Tyrone in the North; her mother, about her family's ancestral home in Mayo. We spoke about her father's experiences in the Ancient Order of Hibernians and about my recollections of Irish Family Days at Navy Pier in Chicago. All the while, glancing at her, it was not hard to imagine the Colleens and Brendans we might raise together.

Today, waiting to see her again, I am happy to have the chance to travel with her to Ireland. We will spend four days in Oxford and London to ring in the New Year, then hop on the train and ferry to the land of Yeats, Wilde, and Shaw. The past few weeks have been exhilarating and exhausting, and we are looking forward to slowing down and being in each other's company.

But when I am honest with myself, I realize that I'm also slightly uneasy. A month traveling alone—no problem; it gave me the chance to sit and explore the world in companionship with my own thoughts. But I've never spent twelve days with just one person, and I don't know what we'll talk about. I mean, we have spent some wonderful time together since last spring. We have spoken words of deep truth to each other, the truth of real love that even now I find startling. This time last year I was ready to live as a bachelor, and a few months later, after attending a concert together, I heard myself saying to her that I hoped one day we could be married. I'm only twenty! But I meant it then, and I still mean it. But what do people talk about when they're married?

She is here, she is here, in the flesh, I can touch her, I can see her eyes and swim in them. When she came off the plane yesterday, even tired and jet lagged, she never looked lovelier. I have so much to tell her, so much detail to share about the things I wrote in the countless letters I sent her during the past three months. And I want to hear everything about what her life has been like—how is grad school? What are the classes like? the people? the new ideas she's encountering? What is she thinking about next year, when she'll get her degree? What about after that? (My God, does she still love me? Will she want to be with me after that?)

"I've really missed you," she says. (I exhale.)

"Me too. I'm so happy to see you again. I've got so much to tell you." Away we go. I tell her about the first arrival in London in October, the circuitous path to Oxford, the completely lost luggage for a weekend, the settling into tutorials, the lecturer who dressed like he lived in the eighteenth century, the rowing on the Isis, the formal dinners, the Common Room conversations, the concerts in medieval chapels, Latin Mass at Saint Aloysius, the bike rides into medieval towns, the Bodleian Library, fencing, the University Sermon at St. Mary's, and so much more. In telling her about my experiences, I enjoy each one all over again. I want her to know everything I've been thinking about while we've been apart. She too recounts everything: the difficult reading, her classmates, her new roommates, the spiritual life, her second-guessing whether she should have done Jesuit Volunteer Corps instead, the papers, the anticipated counseling practicum. In the hour it has taken to ride the bus from London out to Oxford, we have covered a lot of ground. I begin to wonder what the next week and a half will look like if we've just covered three months in a matter of an hour. I have a moment of worry, wondering what we will do to pass the time—until she senses it and reassures me that she's not here to be entertained; she just wants to be with me.

There have been times when, in her presence, I feel too young, and this is one of them. I feel like the kid who needs to be moving constantly—I, who has just spent weeks roaming around

Europe and who has been confronted with the *David*'s lesson about impatience. Her reassurance is the voice of one who is wiser than I, who understands that the reason a person travels is not to consume information about places, but rather to share the experience with someone you love. She has put me at ease; I am here with her now, and we will share our experiences with each other and make some memories together.

I will show her some of what I have loved here, but there is too much. What I really want is for her to stay here with me, to walk with me through Christ Church Meadow every day, to visit the botanical gardens or to listen to evensong at St. Aldate's, to wander through the Ashmolean Museum and take in a lecture. I want to study with her, talk about theology and write essays, celebrate after our eight wins at the Torpids Regatta. I just want her to be with me. These couple of days will have to be simply a glance into my world, a short peek into what has become for me my whole life. What will she think when she sees it? Will she see a confident, brilliant young man, a student at one of the world's great universities, an athlete and a promising intellect, a citizen of the world? Or will she see the truth, the real me, the one who is just flying at breakneck speed in the hope that moving fast will somehow get me to where I'm supposed to be?

See Question 5 p. 136

When we were in Rome, Anne had observed that I always walked faster than everyone else, and asked how in the world my beloved could keep up.

"I slow down for her," I answered.

We spend New Year's Eve in Trafalgar Square. I feel as though there ought to be some sort of formal proclamation that she and I have rung in the New Year together, that this full calendar year will be the first of many. Here, after the countdown, I ask time to slow down and wait for us, to allow us to hold this memory with great care. I know how quickly life can move—my first term already a memory, more than half my college career over, careening toward the next thing, whatever that might be. At least I'm with her now. But I need to take mental images and record them in my journal; I don't want the days and weeks and months to slip by without my taking in fully every experience.

Soon we will depart for Dublin. By now it's occurred to me that I've subjected her to an itinerary that has a single page, with a single line written in large letters: Keep Moving and See as Much as You Can. We traveled from London to Oxford and roamed there for a couple of days, then came back to London to do our touristy best: Westminster, St. Paul's, the Tower, the Roman Wall, Harrods, and of course our brief taste of high culture, the performance of *The Nutcracker* at Covent Garden. These have been very good days; we have never had the luxury of extended time together. If I had the money, I think we would stay in one place, do a lot less moving around, and talk. She makes me think differently about what I want to do with my time.

For now, I am content to be here with her. Like seldom before in my life, I can say that there is nowhere else in the world I'd rather be than right here. What a change from two years ago, when I had half-convinced myself that I'd be a lifelong bachelor. The truth is that I feel free when I am with her—she elicits from me conversations that I would never otherwise have, inviting me to pay attention to parts of my life that I couldn't have even named. Once upon a time I conceived of friendship as having someone to play sports with—that's certainly what it felt like as a kid. Now, she is teaching me a new meaning of friendship, one that I am finding both difficult and yet also gratifying. I am a poor conversationalist; I do not have the skill that she has in drawing people out of themselves and sharing their lives. I respond to her with great interest, but still find myself unable to ask the kinds of rich questions that she asks me. But I am paying attention to the way her mind works, and may yet surprise her.

"What are you hoping for this year?" she asks me.

"More time with you," I answer. This is the truth, but I have learned the art of the clever answer, the I-have-a-quick-mind-and-can-amuse-you answer; it is a skill that developed at home over the years. My family laughs well, but has not always conversed well.

She smiles, knowing that I mean what I've said, and still looks for the real answer, the answer that will emerge not from the persona that I have honed over the years, the everything-is-great-and-I'm-on-top-of-the-world mask, the one I didn't even realize I was wearing. She has asked me a question, offered herself in her words with outstretched hands, and I have merely slapped those hands with verbal high fives, and a laugh. She looks at me pensively. People are moving all around the square in the euphoria of the holiday; she remains fixed even as I glance around at the goings-on. I try again.

"I've been thinking about what I'll do this summer; I have no idea yet, but I want to stay in New England because I can't stand the idea of being separated from you again. And I'm thinking about my thesis next year, and who will direct it and what I'll write on. And I'm thinking about grad school—about master's and doctoral work and what I'll need to do for applications in the fall. And I'm thinking about the Head of the Charles and how I want to get our eight ready, since it'll be my last chance while in college . . ." The words are now pouring out, each expressed concern representing hours of conversations we'll have as time goes on. Suddenly I'm feeling overwhelmed. There are forces shaping my life over which I have little control.

She sees it in my face. Her cheeks are rosy from the cold, and a breeze is blowing her long, luscious, ruddy-tinged light brown hair into her face, sometimes obscuring those eyes. I want to put my hands upon that face, as if the touch might help me understand the mind behind it. Her expression is no longer the light-hearted grin she showed after the New Year's countdown; on her forehead are lines showing concern, and her eyebrows are turned ever so slightly upward. "You don't have to worry about these things alone," she says, perfectly. I know there aren't easy answers, but her reassurance is exactly what I need to hear. She has come on this ride with me, a ride I wish I could control (part of me wondering why she's chosen to take it with me), and I need to hear that even though it's hard she still wants to be here with me. "Let's talk more tomorrow, OK?"

"We've got plenty of time, thank God." I understand something at that moment, something which I suppose ought to have been obvious at some earlier point in my life. It's that there is something wonderful about talking with someone who loves you, about exploring with that person the things in your life that might otherwise go unnamed and unacknowledged. I think about how quickly I move in my daily life, how much I want to live out every moment, especially here in England, where time will go quickly. And I thank God for that energy, for that thirst to seize every day. But I also now wonder whether in my zeal I am living a mile wide and an inch deep—not unlike my recent trip, where I saw everything for a few minutes before rushing off to see something else. Maybe one reason why I love her is that she allows me to pause, to savor, appreciate the things in my life that otherwise would be shelved behind the next experience.

Dublin has been a different experience altogether. Yes, there has been sightseeing, but less of it. There's been movement, but at a slower pace than before. We have taken our time; we have digested and conversed and explored together. I could do this every day. I'm sorry to have to leave tomorrow. It reminds me that soon she'll be on the plane headed home.

We have been staying with the Barretts, a delightful older couple who live in a suburb outside the city, where Mr. Barrett works as a member of the Dáil Éireann, the Irish Parliament. He was good enough to show us around Leinster House and suggest some things to see in the city. His dear wife has been hospitable and lovely to us, even in spite of the fact that it must be a lot of trouble to put up two young tourists. We have spent much of our time wandering around the city, seeing historical sites and museums, neighborhoods and pubs. The weather has at times been wretched, making us feel gloomy but thankful to be together. For me at least, there is something about being gloomy in the presence of the one you love that beats even having a good time alone.

A couple of days ago we spent a good amount of time at Trinity College, and in particular gazing upon the Book of Kells. This, the most famous of the medieval illuminated gospels, is a marvel to see firsthand. At a certain moment, though, I began to wonder whether she shared my fascination. Would she have chosen to come here—for that matter, had she enjoyed the other sites I've seen in the past month? My travel had been so much on my own whim, but I began thinking more and more about whether I'd just been subjecting her to my unusual tastes in tourism. As we left Trinity and walked toward St. Stephen's Green, I tried to broach the subject.

"What did you think?" she asked.

"Wow—even more amazing in real life."

Old habits die hard. We walked several more steps before I realized that I'd done it again, given a perfunctory answer when she was hoping that a juicy open question like the softball she'd just lobbed might start a heart-to-heart conversation. She knows I love literature, and the history of scripture, and monasticism, and the medieval period, and all things Irish—and my response to her question was all of seven words. And one of them was an exclamation. But fortunately, this time I realized it and was able to change course.

"What amazes me when I look at something like that is just the patience—the sheer willingness to sit with a single image on a page for hours and hours, making each word, each face, each knot absolutely perfect. What must that have been like, when somewhere outside their doors were Celtic warriors fighting off hordes of Viking raiders? What drew young men into the monasteries to labor for their entire lives with pens and brushes and ink? You have to believe it's the way you worship God." I paused and then asked, "What about you? What did you think?"

"It was beautiful," she said earnestly. "It's easy to see the source of my parents' taste in art!" This made me smile. In the times I've visited her folks' place, it was very clear that if it had a Celtic knot in it, or was Irish in any way, then it belonged in the china cabinet. There was Belleek and Waterford; Claddagh symbolism; and Celtic knots everywhere.

I became more specific. "Let me know if there's something you'd really like to do while we're here. I don't want you to feel like I have to call all the shots."

"I know. We just have to be a little careful with money." It stung to hear this. I wish I were the kind of guy who could really take care of her—take her out to a nice restaurant, maybe pay for a tour of the city, stay in a nice hotel—but the reality is that it's stressful on the budget even to eat fast food. I suddenly had a panicked feeling that we'd be bored just sitting around the

Barretts' and that she would see me as having dragged her into something she hadn't bargained for.

She did not come from a wealthy family, and I knew that money was a sensitive subject. It was, I think, the thing that terrified me the most last spring when I had the inner turmoil over whether I could tell her that I loved her. What could I give her? What was I asking her to be part of? Transience, waiting until I finished my degrees, living on next-to-nothing? And here— she'd just flown across the Sargasso Sea to be with me, and I couldn't even give her a decent place to sleep for a few days.

See Question 6 p. 137

She called me back to the present. "Look at those lovely houses!" She had a cute smile as she pointed to some Georgian doorways, the kind you see on posters entitled "The Doors of Dublin." And lo, as I looked up, I saw a store named O'Farrell's. A sign!

She chose to come here, I reassured myself. *She is perfectly capable of making decisions about her life. She is smart and talented, a graduate student who could be doing other things with other people. But she wants to be with me, and she knows exactly what she is getting.* (Why? I began to doubt. But I loved her for it.)

"Shall we head to Bewley's for some tea?" I asked. I knew what the answer would be, of course, since tea was a regular ritual in the O'Farrell home. Fine restaurants, no—but missing tea was altogether wrong while we were in Dublin. As her mother was fond of saying: "We may not have much money, but we know how to live right."

During our days in Dublin, our conversations ranged widely: I shared with her more how much I loved Oxford, how much I loved my tutorial on Saint Augustine and my beginning Greek, how much I was looking forward to Torpids. She spoke about her counseling curriculum and the anticipation of her practicum.

We talked about Irish literature and politics, about our favorite memories of things Irish back home. We thought about what it would be like to live there and to really see the country, knowing how much we were missing by confining ourselves to the big city. I resolved that sometime in the future we would have to come back and see the Ring of Kerry, the Cliffs of Moher, and the towns in Mayo and Tyrone, which are home to some of the ghosts of our families' pasts. This will be the beginning of a much longer memory, one that we will one day share with our children.

Over many conversations we began hatching the plan for the family we would build together, and what we would take from our respective pasts and what we wished to create new for the life we were composing in our minds. Perhaps it is the fact that being on Irish soil makes us nostalgic for a past we've never known for ourselves, but one that has nevertheless been so much a part of our growing up, not unlike a relative who had died just as we were born. I think about my great-grandfather Christopher, about whom my great-aunt Eileen has often spoke warmly and tenderly. I imagine him as a young man like me, no doubt wondering how he might secure an income upon landing at Ellis Island, likely hoping that one day he might have a wife and family. His was the courageous departure from Newtownstewart, just north of Omagh—what dreams did he bring with him? What anxieties did he experience about carrying on the family name? Whatever they were, I imagine that they aren't too far removed from those I am contemplating. Here I am, a Muldoon returned to the sod from which my family sprang; and here is she, an O'Farrell and a Bergin by blood; both of us part of the diaspora, having inherited the success story that so eluded our forebears who were wedded to the land itself.

What will be the plot of our story? From firsthand gatherings of my extended family I've learned that we Irish are storytellers. And the part of the story that I know is emblematic of so many others that shaped the parishes and voting blocs of cities like Chicago, Boston, Philadelphia, and New York. It is a story of family helping family, parishioners helping their own, to achieve the American dream. My great-grandfather was the son of a bread porter; I am studying to become a college professor. What, then, for our children? Will our story be one of spoiled third- and fourth-generations whose parents and grandparents did all the hard work, and who will populate the over privileged campuses of today's status-quo factories? Or will our family story be one of diaspora and return, perhaps my children helping rebuild a stagnant Irish economy after their studies in international finance? Or will it be a story of discontinuity, the old sod being a place that their father had heard stories about as a child, but which in latter days is little more than one spot among many on a world map? I cannot begin to answer these questions. I can only hope, with her, to allow our pasts to be the roots that enable our children to grow strong and free.

Tomorrow we leave, and then we will have to say good-bye again. But this time it's different. We will part with the beginnings of a plan to be created over the next few years, a plan that makes everything different and purposeful. We are the sculptors now, and I have never felt more certain that what creation emerges will be beautiful.

4

How Love Opens Up a Life (Spring, 1991)

If I must keep busy until the next time we see each other, at least I am in a place where keeping busy is enjoyable and interesting. The weeks have passed quickly since the beginning of the term, and I've been in the odd position of both wishing for time to move quickly and hoping that it will move slowly so that I can enjoy it. I want to see her again, but I know that when my time here is over in June, I'll miss this place and all it's given me.

My life is one of constant movement; I feel an urgency to squeeze everything out of the time left. In this tug between blessing and longing I am committing myself to regular prayer for the first time as an adult. Not long ago, Campion Hall—the Jesuit house here—advertised an opportunity to undertake the Spiritual Exercises of Saint Ignatius of Loyola, under the guidance of a spiritual director. I jumped at the chance. I'm a product of Jesuit education twice over and am familiar enough with Ignatian spirituality enough to know that it suits my temperament. Back in November, I went with a group of students on retreat to Worth Abbey in Sussex; it was my first experience in a Benedictine monastery. And while I loved the chance to pray with the monks—reciting the Liturgy of the Hours was a satisfying sanctification of time—I realized that it was a prayer life that, while nourishing for my period of retreat, was not in the end something that my active life could fully engage over the long term. I am drawn to learn more about Ignatian spirituality because I have always perceived Jesuits as men most like who I want to become— intelligent, attentive to the poor, hard-working, ordinary men rooted in a spiritual discipline. "Men for Others," as the motto at Loyola Academy put it.

There are a couple dozen of us who have met regularly during Lent and Easter to do the Exercises. I was matched up with a Scottish Jesuit scholastic, Chris, who is a perfect guide for me. Without being overbearing or condescending, he's helped me learn how to pray. He listens well and offers suggestions for how to use biblical texts in prayer. I'm surprised that the process has been as flexible as it has; I guess I imagined that the Jesuits had a really strict and regimented prayer life. I've thrown myself into it; for the past six weeks or so I've not missed a single day of prayer, committing an hour to it each day.

What has captured my attention most is the way Chris has suggested using imagination in prayer. There have been several times over recent weeks when this method has really gotten me thinking about what God is up to. For example, I was praying about Jesus feeding the five thousand, reading the text closely, and what popped out was Jesus' command to the disciples, "You give them something to eat." I'd never noticed it before; but in prayer, I imagined myself as one of the disciples and Jesus speaking this to me directly. I was unnerved by this command; my reaction was defensive: "You're the messiah, here, not me!" But as I continued to pray, I found myself listening more and more to the way that Jesus was inviting me to be the agent that brings about God's will, and it made me feel energized.

Another time I was praying over the story of Zaccheus, imagining myself in his place, running this way and that just to get a look at Jesus, then climbing a tree so I could finally see over the crowd. It was a vivid picture and allowed my emotions to get hold of the story in ways they hadn't before.

This whole process has helped me start really feeling in prayer—not just thinking, which I tend to do too much. I brood and consider and try to work things out in my head. This has been an an experience of listening to God with the ears of my heart more than with the ears of my head. And there is a close parallel to the way I am developing in my relationship with Sue. I think less, feel more, and listen more carefully.

I decided early on not to bring a camera; pictures seem too precise, too limiting—how can they capture the richness of an emotional memory? That is what I have been cultivating: memories of what I have felt while here, impressions upon my heart by people and places and experiences. The Exercises have helped me become more aware of these movements; I have become more thankful for the daily gifts of simple things like food and friendship. Sometimes I am just overwhelmed at the blessings that ordinary days hold for me while here—being able to read in beautiful surroundings, like the Bodleian Library or the College Quad; taking a walk with views of fields and spires; engaging in conversation with interesting people.

Perhaps the greatest challenge has been the practice of coming to understand the intricacies of this burgeoning emotional life. I move from grace to grace, even while my mind often wanders back to her. "This is beautiful!" I will exclaim silently, then lamenting, "How I wish I could share it with her." I will experience gratitude and sorrow, euphoria and lament, exultation and longing at the same time, and ask God where in the world these different movements are supposed to point me. I am coming to understand that the coexistence of these opposing feelings mean that I look in vain for a perfect feeling, a perfect experience—at least without her.

I have been tested. The distance is hard; the absence sometimes stings, and I wonder whether I haven't romanticized the whole thing. I love her; but sometimes now I wonder if I'm like Saint Augustine in the *Confessions* when he wrote that he was in love with love. I read that book as a freshman, and I remember thinking that there was something incredibly astute about that observation. Do I love her, or the feeling of being in love with her? Am I idolizing her? But I call to mind our conversations over the spring, the summer, and the winter break in Dublin. We are sober about what is in front of us; we have talked honestly and forthrightly about what we want out of a life together, and have decided that it is very much worth waiting for. Could I ever find someone else like her?

The truth is that over the past months my friendship with one of the women here is starting to make me nervous. Amy is sweet and understands that I am attached; she was there the day I returned from Rome, and knows how much I couldn't wait to meet Sue. She is a good person and would never seek to hurt anyone. But I know we are attracted to each other; our conversations are easy and engaging. We like spending time together, even though it has almost always been in a group.

See Question 7 p. 137

The one exception was the time I got tickets for a concert at the Sheldonian Theater, and I asked Amy to go. At the time, my thought was innocent enough: I knew she would enjoy it, as she was a music lover; and I figured that it was a good way to spend an otherwise quiet evening. Ironically, after getting off the water with my crew that day, Blair, the ruddy New Zealander who was the team's captain, suggested we all head out to the pub. I was sorry to miss the opportunity, since we were just getting to the point of really coming together as a team in preparation for Torpids. But I said that I'd already made plans for that evening. Blair saw through my thin excuse and made sure the others knew about it. "Don't tell me it's for a *woman*, mate!" he said with mock contempt. Sheepishly, I admitted it. Since dating was a long-dead institution back home, it didn't occur to me until that instant that I'd created a situation that looked suspiciously like a date. I felt a moment of panic: "What would Sue think if she saw us?" But I did not dwell on it, feeling that out of fairness to Amy it was possible for us to go as friends.

She looked beautiful that evening; we both enjoyed the concert and the conversation and the short walk back to the college. But my imagination was working overtime for the sake of some discernment. What was I to do? On the one hand, there was the foundation of a life that Sue and I had begun to construct while in Dublin, built on several months of shared experiences, longings, and hopes. On the other hand, there was the new desire to explore possibilities with Amy, a woman I found attractive and exciting.

One thing was clear: this was not the time to make a decision. The heightened emotions accompanying the evening were not conducive to wise considerations. As we approached the college, I decided to keep our good-bye simple. There was a part of me that wanted to kiss her good night, but that it was not the part of me that ought to have the final word. "I'll walk you to your building just to be safe," I said. "But I've got to finish some reading before my tutorial tomorrow morning." She looked genuinely happy; and after I saw her to the door, I wrenched myself away, and went to pray.

It was a profound experience of prayer, of bringing what I was thinking and feeling into conversation with God and asking for a little clarity. I am attracted to Amy; I did not choose to be, but I know I am. I enjoy talking with her, I enjoy her laugh; I enjoy the fact that we can talk about literature and music. I feel happy when I am around her. I asked God where he was in these feelings—he who had created me capable of them, capable of finding myself attracted to another woman even as I held close the memory of my beloved. What, I asked, was I to do with even the more basic yet powerful desire for physical presence with someone I found exciting? Could I bring this new feeling into harmony with those that I've developed over the past year, or was it out of place completely, a feeling that needed to be silenced?

The memories that Sue and I had cultivated over the past several months, and the plans that we hatched back in January, still gave me great hope and consolation. I dwelt on these feelings for a while. Yes, I thought, she is far away, but what we have shared and what we hope for together have carved out a place in my heart that is deep and rich. These are not temporary feelings; they have been tested already and have shown me that they will deepen and mature. I realized, of course, that integrity demanded a choice: I could not sustain this relationship by entertaining a new one. I considered what it would mean to close the Sue chapter of my life out of hope for what might emerge with Amy. Immediately, imagining this possibility brought feelings of regret, pain, and loss, similar to what I felt when I ended the relationship with Laura. But these feelings were much worse. The idea of ending my relationship with Sue was so horrible that I couldn't consider it any further. At the same time, the idea of not starting a relationship with Amy made me feel a loss, but a softer one—a disappointment, a sadness, perhaps simply a missed opportunity. And I understood that someone like her—someone so alive, so lovely—would have no trouble finding someone who could love her as much as I loved Sue.

I emerged from prayer convicted, even as I acknowledged the difficulty of my decision. My friendship with Amy would remain platonic. And my relationship with Sue underwent another change. I had chosen her once again, taking a risk, offering her my heart in a quiet way that she might never really understand. In my physical training over the years I had experienced the satisfaction of sacrificing one thing in order to have another, and this decision about my relationships felt similar. I felt stronger and more resolved that I was doing the right thing, both for Sue and for me.

See Question 8 p. 138

As it turned out, I needed that resolve not long after.

The occasion was a college party in the Junior Common Room following Eights Week. The previous four days had been an incredible high for me, as our boat had raced well on each of them. The weeks leading up to the races had been up and down; the eight was not the same that had raced in Torpids—the fastest boat I'd ever been in—and so we had a good bit of work to do in order to be ready for the competition. But the week before the races, things came together nicely. Our starts had improved dramatically, and we had achieved that feeling of swing together that promised good racing. Sure enough, our races were strong—particularly the last one, when we made up two lengths on a boat that started two places in front of ours. We did not win blades—the rare accomplishment of overtaking four boats in four days—but I went home from the final race riding an adrenaline rush, a sense of pride, accomplishment and relief, after months of hard training. Eights Week itself was like nothing I'd ever seen; it was pageantry and ritual and parties and traditions all centered around the college boathouses. I felt like a celebrity as our eight pushed off from the dock for the final race; it seemed the entire university community had turned out to watch us that day. Our return to the dock after a stunning race was cause for great celebration.

The parties around the town were something between a national holiday and a sports championship; everyone seemed happy and alive, at least to me. I can't remember ever feeling so on top of the world. My whole body was alive; I enjoyed the feeling of my heart pounding, my senses attuned to the things going on around me, my muscles tensed with the excitement of having performed well. At our college, the drinks flowed freely, and pretty soon everyone was feeling happy and mellow. For once I regretted a little that I wasn't a drinker. I'd just never developed the habit, mainly because of my training schedule. But this night it seemed like everyone was able to enjoy themselves. Everyone was telling stories, enjoying the music, playing games, having a great time.

Amy was in the middle of it all. She had an ease in social situations that added to her attractiveness, and she laughed and chatted throughout the evening at the center of the party. She had been casting glances my way several times, and her body language was inviting. With the waning of her usual inhibitions, she became more and more obvious, draping her hand across my arm or shoulders.

At a certain point I noticed two other men hovering near her as others headed home. They were clearly drunk and looked as if they might take advantage of the situation. So I stayed near Amy through the evening until well past midnight, when everyone began staggering back to their respective rooms. The wolves were following Amy back to her room when she looked at me somewhat sleepily, with a half smile, and asked, "Are you going to help me keep my chastity belt on?"

I'd never before had so obvious an invitation. But under the circumstances I knew that her safety was at stake. So I continued to walk her back to her room; I didn't answer her question, even though a part of me wanted to take her back to my own room.

The night ended innocently enough after I assumed that she was safe in her room. I went back to my own, far from able to sleep, even after the exhaustion of the past several days.

I have learned much from the discipline of training. The most obvious lesson that I sat with that very early morning was about delayed gratification, and the knowledge that my body can tolerate immediate discomfort for the sake of what my mind has seized upon as a goal. Many times over the past three years I have denied myself the immediate comfort of rest or food, arising at 5:00 a.m. to run down to the boathouse, and maintaining a careful diet free of junk food. And so I am no stranger to delayed gratification; the joy of the past day's race was a testament to the deep wisdom of leaving nothing to chance and of making hard decisions about forgoing temporary pleasures for the sake of something greater and more lasting.

And yet the knowledge that I had often benefited from this discipline was little comfort to me then—I felt very alone. Underneath my skin I felt blood rushing, nerves firing, muscles breathing in the energy of the past day, and like never before I felt as though my cells were reaching out for human contact, in mutiny against my conscience. There is something deeply mysterious about the way sexual imagination functions, often quite apart from the well-ordered workings of reason. What gave me comfort was that even in spite of what might have transpired with Amy that evening, my imagination was focused entirely on wanting to feel the embrace of the woman I had already chosen.

The paradox of the sculpture is that it emerges beautiful precisely because it has been submitted to the violence of the chisel again and again. On this night I felt that violence, a violence against my emotions and my body. I wrote a long letter to Sue, expressing how much I wished she were with me, how much I wanted to feel her touch and be with her in person. The distance, I wrote, has been hard. I am not in love with love, for if I were I could not tolerate this separation. I am in love with *her*—the whole of her, not only our conversations or our shared ideas or our plans for the future, but the very person whose image I encounter in my dreams so often. I miss her face, her hair, the way she holds my fingers between hers, the small of her back, the shape of her neck and shoulders when she asks me to rub them. What I miss is the whole of her that stands before me as a woman, the whole package.

For months now I have read her letters—beautiful letters, through which we have explored so many contours of each other's mind—but these letters also bring into sharp relief how much I want again to be able to touch her. Beneath my skin there is a wisdom rooted in the desire to know everything about her, to really *know* her, as in the biblical euphemism. Now I understand this knowledge very differently: it is no longer the crass hormone-driven cravings of adolescence, which in all honesty still show up from time to time. Instead, I have sensed a more deeply rooted desire, one which comes before reason and understanding, but which is governed by a logic that I can describe only as corporeal. Pascal once wrote that the heart has its reason which reason can never know; he was only partly right. The body, too, has its reason, a desire to encounter another person without falsehood or façade, without the posturing of a contrived persona: in a word, naked. My body was in those quiet hours laboring to state its case, and how I wished then to be able to render both judgment and reward in another encounter with her.

5

WHEN TWO LIFE STRUGGLES MERGE INTO ONE (SUMMER, 1993)

When I am older I will look back on the past three years and likely consider it a short time, but today it feels as if we have condensed a lifetime of memories into them. Today I am not the same person I was at nineteen, when I took the risk of revealing my heart to Sue. We have grown together in this time, suffered together, built a castle of hope together that now we'll begin to inhabit as a married couple.

Life since Oxford has been a mix of purposeful necessity and blind trust, in both the artistry of a loving God and the resolve of a beautiful woman. My senior year back in Boston flew by, punctuated by the consolations of short reunions with her. I wrote my thesis on the Christian understanding of the theology of the Trinity, a project which grew out of the research I had begun in Oxford. I enjoyed writing and looked forward to carrying on my studies in graduate school. She labored through her own graduate studies under the very mistaken assumption that she had to keep up with everyone else, only to discover by the end that she, together with a friend, had achieved the highest overall scores in their program. By spring of last year we came to a point of both excitement and concern; it was time to make a decision about what would be next.

The decision hinged on where I would continue my studies. I had sent out applications to several schools and hoped to receive a scholarship from one of them. In the months since then I'd carried the tension of how the outcome would affect not only my own career hopes, but also the prospects for our eventual wedding. For by the middle of that year it was abundantly clear that it would be pointless to keep putting off what both of us desired. We wanted to be at home with one another.

My, the lifetimes that are contained in fateful letters! The first had been my college acceptance letter—this letter affected the course of the past five years and will continue to leave its imprint on what unfolds from here. The second one was, of course, my acceptance and scholarship to the Candler School of Theology at Emory University, which has now been my home for nearly a year. I will remember it as the place where we began our new life together.

It's a modest beginning, to be sure, living on Farnell Court in Emory's graduate student housing. The honeymoon is over; now begins the work of sanctifying our shared daily life. I feel graced, not only by the deep contentment of being near her now, but also by the events of the past months that have brought us to this point.

The move to Atlanta came together in stages. After my acceptance, she began to look for work opportunities that would justify her own relocation following graduate school. Georgia, it turns out, is one of the worst states for counseling licensure, and yet she is willing to give her professional life a try there. In time, she worked out a living arrangement with some friends who had moved there, and resolved to find whatever work she could—a feasible assumption, even though the reality proved much more difficult. After a summer at her parents' home in Connecticut, spent mostly watching the Summer Olympics and wondering what life might have been like if I had been good enough to make a lightweight eight, we both moved south in late August. After several days of sleeping on the floor at her new place, I eventually rented a small bedroom in a house on Oxford Road, just off campus. It was cheap and convenient, but had the significant drawback of being only periodically accessible to her place via public transportation. We saw each other as much as we could, but with the demands of coursework and employment—the latter of which brought a host of headaches and anxieties—our time together was scarce and therefore precious. Stability, or at least a sufficient semblance of it to justify married life, still seemed to be a distant dream.

At some point in those early months, though, we both recognized an important truth: waiting for stability before embarking on marriage was absurd. We were struggling against the assumption that we had to already have our financial and professional lives in order before we could marry; that assumption was one of the unwritten social codes that prevailed among so many of our peers. The implication, it seemed, was that one had to present to the future spouse a "package"—a marriage-ready partner, complete with plans for income, living arrangement, childbearing and raising, job- and chore-sharing, and so on. It was part of the unwritten contract for marriage.

See Question 9 p. 138

I can't say who moved whom in the slow dismantling of this assumption, but it happened. I think we both realized that there would be a lot of hard work before we could walk into the perfect suburban life (a life that holds little attraction for us, anyway), and it made more sense to struggle *together* to build a life, rather than to wait for the perfect moment when it was already a reality. In my own mind, the logic was fairly simple: "I'm working hard and can't wait to marry her; she's working hard and can't wait to marry me. Why not just work hard together and share married life in the meantime?"

Minds made up, we both understood that the plot of our drama was leading to a crucial moment—the proposal. I set the plan in motion.

The plan failed. It was a good plan: pick up the ring from the jeweler, take her out to the Atlanta Ballet to see Tchaikovsky's *Romeo and Juliet*, and walk through a beautiful park to the spot where I would propose to her by giving her a new poem, one which I had wrought carefully over recent weeks in my best calligraphic hand. I had mapped everything out, biking along the route in advance to insure that my choreography was correct. But all three elements of my plan fell through. First, there was a misunderstanding about when I was to pick up the ring; second, the tickets were for Prokofiev's ballet, not Tchaikovsky's; and third, it was an ugly, rainy day, and so walking to the park was out of the question.

Now I understand that of the three problems, the second seems trivial. It seemed more consequential to me on that day. I had been building up that day subtly—"Sunday will be a great day!" I said to her a couple of times, and got the sense she knew what I was talking about. But when on Saturday I realized that I would not have the ring the next day, I was dejected, and so the error about the ballet—no small expense to a graduate student—became magnified. I had hoped to propose after a Tchaikovsky ballet because three years ago I took her to see his *Swan Lake*. It was early spring, when we were still only friends, but she later shared with me that the experience of going from the ballet at the Wang Center in Boston to a stroll in the Public Garden was for her a delightful, peaceful experience, one that made her wonder if there might be something more between us. I had hoped to create a parallel experience to that one, and so the mix-up about the ballet added to my discontent.

This year has been a frustrating one in many ways. I had the usual stresses of graduate school life, with papers and tests and all the rest. I also started part-time work, coaching rowing for Georgia Tech and eventually for Emory—which has meant early mornings on the water, followed by classes. Sue had many stresses in the early months of her work life; the money she earned at positions for which she was overqualified made it necessary for her to seek out supplemental income. Her living situation had its ups-and-downs, too, adding to her stress. Add to all that the fact that we usually only got real time together on weekends, and the picture as a whole added up to a series of frustrating challenges. My disappointment at my failed proposal plan was palpable, and only led her to wonder what in the world was going on.

Things came to a head not long after that. I had finally worked out picking up the ring and carried it with me, not wanting to let it out of my sight. But I hadn't devised a second plan for proposing. On a dreary autumn day, we were venting about all that was making life hard for us. We were back at her place, on a rare occasion when she had the apartment to herself. Her roommates and their babies were out visiting family, and so we could just relax. At some point I remarked how tired she looked.

"Of course I'm tired!" she said, testily. "I've worked sixty hours this past week at the psych hospital and the store. My boss is some nurse who's never studied counseling, I'm doing the same kind of group work I did in grad school, and I'm selling cookware on the side!"

I sucked in my breath. Nothing pains me more than seeing her hurt. But what came out was my own frustration, my own sense that this was somehow my fault, for dragging her along through my studies in stinking theology rather than something normal people do, like law school. "It won't last forever, hon," I said.

"But there are student loans to worry about, not to mention finding a better place to live." I knew that her living arrangement was far from ideal—she had a bedroom in an apartment shared with an entire family, and another friend of theirs was soon to join them.

I was reaching for something to give her hope and came up empty. No immediate plans for money, no way to help her with getting a better foot in the door of her professional life. I could offer her nothing, and it was like a knife in the heart. "Just give it time, sweetie. Everything will be fine, I'm sure."

Her response was filled with emotion. "I just wish I had something I could be sure of!"

God, I did too. In one of those rare moments when my academic life resonated significantly with my personal life, I thought about something we were studying in my class on the Hebrew Scriptures. It was the use of a Hebrew verb that described the cry of the Israelites in the book of Exodus—the cry which God hears when he decides to liberate them from slavery, the verb translated as "cry out" as when the psalmist describes God: "The Lord hears the cry of the poor." This was all very stream of consciousness; I wasn't exactly parsing Hebrew verbs in my mind in the middle of this conversation (though I have to admit it does happen from time to time!) but I was feeling deeply the "crying out" that I heard from Sue. Here was a woman who had followed me south to this new city, giving no heed to the demands of her professional life, and forsaking everything just to be near me. I heard a woman so focused on one thing—marrying me—that she was willing to throw caution to the wind in order to cultivate that dream. When I heard that crying out, I was moved like never before. And what moved in me, among other things, was a realization that three years earlier (it was almost three years to the day when I opened my heart to her the first time) my motivation was almost entirely selfish. *I* had to tell her what *I* was feeling; *I* had fallen in love with her; *I* wanted her to be with *me*.

The only proper response was thankfulness and humility, and the resolve to make her a promise. "I will give you something you can be sure of," I said, running to the other room. I retrieved the ring and the poem from my bag, went back to her, knelt down while looking into her tearstained face, and asked her to marry me.

See Question 10 p. 139

There are only so many emotions that even she is capable of sustaining in a given moment, and I suspect that she was operating then at full capacity. Later she described to me what had been going through her mind.

Oh God is this the moment . . . God what must I look like right now—I must be a wreck . . . God yes! . . . my God what is he thinking, proposing to me in this dreary room on a rainy day . . . yes! yes! . . . this year has been so hard, and the last three years have been so long and now all this will change and we will find our own home, our own space, a place to be together and to come home at night to each other, and there will be no more good- byes or good nights and I can finally stop relying on the fourteen roommates I've had over the past four years and we will make our own rules and oh my God he looks so sweet right now, have I just been crying? Her face, which has never been able to keep anything from me—she would make the most terrible poker player—showed everything, and she barely even had to breathe the word, even though the sound of it was like the hum of a well-ordered universe: "yes."

I am a believer in ritual. I am now halfway to a master of theological studies degree, and have studied the ways that cultures and societies create ritual for the most important moments of their collective lives. I believe in the way that rituals invite us into a drama that is grander than ourselves, reminding us that the profound moments of our lives are part of a still greater narrative of people who have gone before us and people who will come after us, and that in ritual we play small but beautiful roles. And so as I knelt there, assuming the position of a man who humbly asks a woman for her hand in marriage, and as I took the ring and placed it on her finger, I became mindful of another element in the story. Within a few minutes, I called her parents. In my mind this part of the story, perhaps a remnant of a time when a woman's decision was really that of her father, was nevertheless a recognition that they who had loved her so long and so well as a child and as a young adult could offer us their blessing. And a blessing is what I sought: a simple statement that they who always sought her good would embrace her decision, our decision. And so when their excitement on the other end of the phone overflowed and spilled all around the apartment, we grew even happier. "If she didn't marry you soon," her dad observed, "we would have adopted you as our son anyway!"

We had a beautiful spring wedding at St. Ignatius Church next to the Boston College campus, replete with family and friends from many stages of our lives. It was an experience of fullness, of the richness that accompanies joyful celebrations of people who love generously. It was one of a very few times in my life when I can remember wishing to have the faculty of "playback"—being able to pause, rewind, or fast forward through moments, to savor them, appreciate them, relive them, and share them again and again. Some guests we had not seen in a long time, and wished to have more time with them. Others we saw regularly, but wanted to share with them everything we were feeling that day. To all I wanted to show my gratitude for their blessing us by their simple choice to be part of our Cana.

She was transfigured, radiant, exultant, perfect. I wish I could have seen my own face seeing her for the first time that day, both of us stripped of anything resembling pretense and living simply in the pregnant moments of procession, vows, prayers, and recession. Later, amidst the throngs of guests at the reception, she was ever present to me, our new duo representing a moment of stillness in a symphony of celebration. We did not want the day to end; we wanted to relish the great goodness of the event and allow it to impress many memories into the new book of our marriage. And so it was with some good humor that our parents wondered aloud, late into the evening: "What are you still doing here?"

I think we both turned several shades of red at the insinuation. But realizing that in fact they had a point—we did need at some point to exit the room—we said our good-byes, saddened that the day was ending.

6

How Love Blooms into Fascination (Summer, 1993)

There is a difference between seeing a picture of a beautiful church and standing in the nave of the Cathédrale Notre-Dame de Chartres. There is a difference between talking about love and falling deeply in love with the person you desire. There is a difference between analyzing a poem and allowing it to move you because of its beauty. There is a difference between studying a kinetic world of atoms and meditating on a profound and mysterious world charged with grandeur. There is a difference between talking abstractly about the existence or nonexistence of God and listening with great hope for a living God whose whispers become clearer in hindsight, through the tender words of those who love with abandon. And there is a difference between the idea of sex and making love with someone who has promised to love you forever. The reality is deep, rich, expansive, fulfilling, permanent, and memorable; it sculpts a person, shaping his experience and outlook.

The first things that fell away that night, like the tired and useless pages of an old glossy magazine, were the images of sex I had accumulated over the normal course of adolescence. Years before, during our first kiss, I recalled having the feeling that we must have looked like a scene from an old movie, when the leading man and woman finally exchange a passionate kiss as the final scene comes to an end. Later, when I learned that in reality she had felt an awful stiffness in her neck the whole time, having to tilt her head up because I am taller, I realized that the image in my head was unreal and misleading. I learned the habit of crouching down or sitting next to her, so that our kissing wouldn't require her to go to a chiropractor. Similarly, on this night, the need to write a new script, rather than try to rehearse those I had imagined (many, many times) over the past three years became pressingly obvious.

We arrived at the hotel completely spent. The emotion of the day—the past several, really—had taken its toll. We had looked forward to this day for three years, ever since we'd first talked about it after a concert our first summer together. And now the day had come and gone, already sliding into our shared memory. We were husband and wife, and we looked forward with great anticipation to simply being home for one another. I wanted to hold her and carry her into my dreams that night, to simply relish the feeling of never again having to wait before we could begin building a life together.

The feeling of being alone in the room together, lifted by the prayers and well-wishes of so many people we loved, was at once consoling and startling. The waiting had been difficult, and to have finally arrived at this point without regret felt incredibly liberating. And yet I felt something I did not expect: patience. Seeing how tired Sue was, knowing how draining the day and its lead-up had been, I thought it would be best if we simply crashed, and postponed our next memory till the following day.

The feeling was remarkable—I had never previously imagined deferring sex for a moment longer than necessary. But in that room, there were no abstractions; there was Sue, and here was I, and I found myself wanting what was best for her. Of course there was a part of me that desired sex; but that voice was stilled by a louder voice which could simply enjoy our new freedom, and wait patiently for another day.

More remarkable, though, was the moment I could set aside my imagination and simply attune myself to the woman who stood before me. It was at that moment—one I have revisited time and again—that I came to understand, as a bedrock truth, that there is something sadly misleading about "sex," as though it were some kind of abstract experience one could seek. I could articulate it only in the most basic words: "there's only you and me now." No images; no movie scenes; no script. I looked at her like I had never looked at her before: there were no boundaries left to be crossed, no further expectations to fulfill. There were only the two of us, beginning a new chapter of our shared life. She was scared; I was scared; and yet we were facing it together. The moment was—in the most real way I can imagine—holy. It was holy in the sense of being saturated with mystery, suffused with shared love, pregnant with possibility. We prayed, and then embraced the mystery.

Later, in the middle of the night, I awoke. I laughed at the disparity between the image of the "player" and the reality of who I was then—a novice with good intentions and a lot of naïveté, and yet a desire to carry into this new dimension of our relationship the same intensity of care and attention that I showered upon her as often as I could elsewhere. Here was a new area of our life together that invited passionate engagement, and it did not take long to move from humble appreciation to enthusiastic embrace. In this kind of embrace it is easy to understand the old phrase, *With my body, I thee worship.*

Thus evening came, and morning followed—the first day. We were off for a three-day sojourn to a lovely little house on Cape Cod, thanks to the generosity of a mutual friend's parents. The house bore the well-deserved name *Serenity,* perched as it was just steps away from the shore and its regular chorus of wave upon sand. It was an idyllic place to begin a new life, sheltered from both the incursions of well-meaning loved ones and the stresses that still lay before us when we returned to the real world. This pattern—of immersion in something perfect, but finite— has characterized our relationship all along. This latest gift represented a consummation of our early hopes: the opportunity to share unencumbered days newly liberated to explore with each other the plush contours of our imagination. We had no agenda, no place to go, nothing to accomplish, no need for contact with the outside world. It was, in every sense, a retreat.

In my studies over the previous year, I had learned much about the ways that early Christians sometimes went off to the desert to live in extended retreat from the world, some for the rest of their lives. The object of these retreats was the exploration of the inner world and God's presence therein, of the gentle swaying of grace moving a person's will toward some decision about life. Our three days at *Serenity* were like that: freed to enjoy a new chapter in our relationship, we spent long restful hours on the patio overlooking the beach and simply learned how each other felt. Deep satisfaction, thankfulness, joy, relief— all these emotions were swirling around our minds, even as a new one emerged slowly, like a sunrise. It was a vague yet pressing sense that there was more at stake here, a plotline in our common narrative that was only now just beginning to unfold. "We have made it"—this was our shared sensibility of what the previous three years had wrought in us—"and now there is something more." Just as a graduation marks a commencement; we understood that our marriage marked the beginning of something altogether new and challenging. We had reached one station on our shared pilgrimage, but there were certainly more to come.

Our unfolding physical relationship was the yin to our more cerebral, conversational yang. I had little point of reference for the experience, and so appealed to how my years in physical training had affected me. I understood that there was a deep and abiding connection between the physical and the spiritual. It was hard to train when feeling depressed; it was exciting to train when riding a high. A great workout could produce feelings of elation, and a sluggish one could produce lethargy. Even over the first three days we became attuned to the long-lingering consequences of sex, heightening our abilities to attend to the other in the more mundane moments of the day. Did she need a foot rub? Or a shoulder squeeze? Was her expression showing a feeling of sadness or pain? The effects of each new experience were like the reverberations of sound in an acoustically perfect room—waning in sheer strength, but nevertheless beautiful in the way they completed the performance.

See Question 11 p. 139

I became fascinated with her, and could see in the way she looked at me that the feeling was deeply mutual. Not long ago, Sue's brother shared with her how much he marveled at the way I look at her. "It's like you're the only woman in the world to him," he said. In a way, he is right. From those early days of our married life, those days that represented both a culmination of what we had already shared and an anticipation of the shared work of building a life together, we looked at each other with a privileged sight, a transfiguring sight. She summoned from me the desire to be the best possible man I could be for her.

My heart was full. Never before had I known such a pervasive sense of rightness, of being at home in this world. Never before had I felt so right in my own skin, this flesh made word to her, this earthen vessel holding gifts to her that only I could give. She said I made her feel beautiful, sexy, adored, loved; it nearly overwhelmed me. And yet I embraced the feeling, knowing full well that three days do not make a lifetime and that these feelings would remain with me as a cherished memory. Yes—even now, I revisit them, dwell in them, bring them alive again, allow them to draw us into their glow for a while, when we retreat at night from the rest of the world. The constant refreshment of these memories is a source of great consolation, a reservoir of living water from which we continue to draw even in times of desolation.

Some time ago, I visited an Indian reservation where I learned that the indigenous language was only for members of the clan; outsiders would never be taught the language, which had never been written down. How strange, I thought, but now I understand that there can exist an intimate language between people that can never really be shared. Perhaps the sounds can be imitated; perhaps one might come to appreciate elements of the grammar. But the poetry unfolds only within a deep relationship, the reciprocity of unconditional love giving rise to the freedom to self-reveal and other-embrace. During these three days, we taught each other the rudiments of our own sexual language. Its nuances and intonations were elegant and complex: a narrowing or widening of the eyes over breakfast or a finger grazing over the back of my hand during a walk suggested resonances with a conversation from the day before or some yet-unforeseen hope for the future. I became attuned to her in entirely new ways, watching and studying her for hints of what treasures lay submerged beneath the surface of conscious thought. And in so doing, I became aware of depths in my own life that I had never previously explored. How glorious, I thought, that we now have time to travel through these worlds together.

There is a freedom in hope, of looking beyond the demands of the moment to the broader desires which bring joy. We filled our days with hope, the language of hearts rooted in shared prayer for our new common good. I prayed for children, knowing (even amidst my own trepidation) that her heart's desire was to be a mother. She prayed for my studies, knowing that I had set my heart on the academic life. And thus in the course of our conversations there emerged an opaque picture, the contours of which we could only partially discern: a picture of a young family (how many children?) enjoying long summer vacations at home, not wealthy, but together because of the benefit of an academic schedule. It soon became clear to us that the course of the next several years would be measured by the ways that we could move ourselves to make that picture a reality.

7

WHEN REAL LIFE IS LIVED
TOGETHER
(SPRING, 1994)

We have begun to establish the foundation of a daily life, one we have never known. The smallest elements of this life are delectable: making dinner together in our tiny kitchen, watching the small black-and-white TV perched on a box on the hope chest at the end of our bed before drifting off to sleep, being awakened by the train that passes behind our apartment, and feeling the warmth of her skin still within reach. For so long we have longed for the thrill of the ordinary, and so now it's a great joy to possess it. Still, as we look ahead, sobering challenges lie before us, of constructing a life with the usual demands of finding work and income. We have had the great blessing of uninterrupted time to celebrate our new life; now we must begin our work together.

I'm a little uneasy because her work prospects have been poor, thanks to the recession of the past year. My continued studies depend much on Sue finding work. I'm prepared to take off a semester or two and find a job if necessary, but I'm afraid that if I do that, then everything else will be harder to resume later.

Last year I could live my Spartan existence in my little bedroom for a few hundred dollars a month, eating cheap pasta for dinner. My European experience was a lesson in modest living, and I know I can do it. But I can't expect her to live that way. I wish I could provide her with a nicer place to live in, but the truth is that even the graduate student apartments are a stretch on our budget. Back in the spring, I put down a deposit to hold one for the fall, knowing that this option was the cheapest and closest to campus for me. I didn't even have time to see what it looked like. Now that we're here, it feels small and shabby.

Recently Sue raised the question of decorating the place. "I'm thinking about making some window treatments out of fabric that's on sale, and maybe buying some pillows for the couch." She was referring to the piece we'd found at a yard sale for fifty bucks.

"I'm not sure that's the best way to be spending money right now," I said. In my mind, if you can't eat it, it's not a necessity.

That was plainly the wrong approach. "So you're saying that you don't want to do any decorating at all?"

I was on the defensive, even without having intended to be. "No, that's not what I mean—I'm just concerned about the money . . ." I trailed off, seeing the tension in her face.

"So you're comfortable inviting people over with a tablecloth over the window?" It was white, with red, blue, and green flowers, arranged kind of like a curtain. Not bad, I thought, until this moment.

"I guess it just wasn't that high a priority for me," I said, trying to be honest.

See Question 12 p. 140

"It is a priority for me," she said tersely, though keeping her cool. "I can't let people see the place this way. It's different for the woman. You chose this place, but you have to let me decorate it."

I was stung. I was still learning to move into her world as I was inviting her into mine. And with some sadness I also realized that I couldn't (yet?) give her what would allow her to build the world she dreams about. I think I would like it there, but now I am only a poor theology student.

She has every right to be angry. She's the one who has taken a step backward in her professional life to be here in Atlanta with me, and with a tough job market she's still looking for a permanent position. I'll start coaching again soon, which will help, but I'm going to try to find something else part-time. The stress of uncertainty is hard; there is a lingering part of me that wonders whether it was right to invite her into my world when my prospects are modest for the foreseeable future. I want to see her happy, but I don't have the resources to offer even a decent home with window treatments.

The best I can do right now is work toward the long-term, which means finishing this master's degree so I can at least get a good teaching job in a Catholic school. Perhaps if things work out I can get a scholarship to a doctoral program next year—I've got to get on the applications before too long—and she can find something that better suits her professional life. But that's all a long way off.

The situation has made me profoundly aware of the need to cultivate and sustain a prayer life, because at times the enormity of these challenges is more than I can easily handle. I will keep rowing, but a little wind in my sails wouldn't hurt.

The difference a year makes. Last April we were in the throes of planning a long-distance wedding; our entire winter and spring were consumed with navigating the vast jungle of wedding planning. I was plugging away through my coursework and coaching. She was juggling jobs she could find while trying to stay sane in her living situation. Neither of us had any money, we couldn't see each other that much, and we were just trying to struggle through the semester.

Now, peace, thanks be to God. I wasn't sure it would happen after the move into the apartment, when for many weeks she was still having trouble finding some decent work. I sold shoes at Rich's department store for a while and hated it, but actually started making money. Somehow I managed to work out the hours with my course schedule and was still able to start the semester on time, and did just fine with very full days. Awake before sunrise, coach the Emory crews on Stone Mountain Lake—a beautiful place to be, always lifting my spirits—then breakfast and classes all morning, studying and writing papers in the afternoon, many evenings at the store, coming home late at night. But she was there! The routine of coming home late to see her was almost too good to believe. Eating ice cream and watching TV together were, for the season, the definition of contentment, even amidst the strain of tight finances.

In late September we rejoiced when she finally landed a good job as a youth minister at the Cathedral of Christ the King. It was a professional position, one that would pay her a salary that would enable us to successfully pay bills every month. Before long we even found ourselves at a car dealership, purchasing our first vehicle, a sweet little red wagon that we duly named the Buggy. Some day there will be child seats in it! The plan was beginning to unfold.

When one is married to a youth minister, one is inevitably also a youth minister. And when one is also, coincidentally, a graduate student in theology, one tends to spend a great amount of time at his wife's workplace. It was there that I witnessed a new dimension of her personality, which emerged as a necessity of her leadership position. It was a Sunday evening, when the youth events usually took place. She was calling the rather crowded room to attention—or rather, asking me with my best stentorian voice to do so—after which she began explaining what would be happening that evening, and giving some reflection on cultivating one's prayer life. I stood at the back of the room in amazement, in large part because it was remarkable to me at that moment that there was any side of her that I did not already know. Yet when I thought about it further, it occurred to me that even over the course of four years, we had not enjoyed a great deal of uninterrupted time together, and so it was really little surprise that there were some things about her I had yet to learn.

I was attracted to this new expression of her personality; it made me happy to think about all the gifts that she had. And it made me even happier to realize that this is my wife. This is a person whose mystery I will never exhaust, who will surprise me again and again over the course of the coming years. I, a person who explores the inner life and who has been drawn into studying the ways people talk about God, who appreciates something of the depths of our conscious and unconscious thoughts, I who am a mystery to myself, understand anew how much more she, whom I have loved passionately for these four years, is even more a mystery to me. This realization was as brief as it was profound. When we went home that night, I tried to express to her what I'd realized, finding it difficult to locate the words. "You were amazing," I said, somewhat blandly. "I've never seen that side of you before." How could I give words to my glimpse into the mystery of my beloved?

Within a short time the disparate uses of my energies, in married life and in theological studies, reached a confluence in my decision to write my master's thesis on the theology of marriage. The decision was obvious, in my mind: my married life was like

See Question 13 p. 140

a lab in the intricacies of the spiritual life, and I wanted the time to explore its meaning. I was fascinated by the ways that our relationship summoned from me pure wonder, thanksgiving, joy, but also, at times, sacrifice, suffering, and dejection. This relationship was where I discerned the soft whispers of God in the voice of my beloved. It was like a seed that began to grow as our relationship grew. Its fruit was patient listening to her when she expressed frustration at her professional life, joy when she shared a personal triumph or excitement, and compassion when she shared a past hurt. Even now, after four years, when my heart beats faster upon seeing her at the end of a long day, or when she kisses me to let me know she is thinking of me, I become mindful of a loving God whose presence she manifests to me. Yet I also have become more aware of my limitations; I want to love her back, to be the face and hands of God to her, but sometimes find myself too exhausted physically or emotionally to do so. Here, in the back-and-forth of the everyday, is the holy ground upon which we dance—we who are imperfect and sluggish creatures—yet who nevertheless live and move in the presence of a God who every moment makes us capable of loving each other in new ways every day, grace upon grace upon grace.

The immersion in intellectual study of the history of Christian reflection upon marriage, especially that of Thomas Aquinas, whose work provided the focus for my writing, was like engaging in a long conversation with others who, like me, wanted to understand where God was in married life. Why was my heart moved to marry her, when once upon a time I wanted to be a bachelor philosopher? What in me made it possible to trust her, to sacrifice to be with her, to orient my whole life around being near her always? Where did these desires come from? Did I choose them freely, or were they built into my DNA? Would they remain with me? Did I need to cultivate them carefully, lest they be choked off by weeds, or would they grow no matter what? The process was as much self-examination as it was study of ancient texts. Over the course of the last several months, I have developed not only a facility in reading medieval theology, but I have also come to a deeper appreciation of the dynamic of God's grace in the ordinariness of our life. And I am profoundly thankful; there are nights when I come home after pondering these things and simply being amazed at the world in front of me.

I will hand in the thesis in a couple of weeks, and only a few weeks after that we will be leaving Atlanta altogether. The decision was not an easy one; we talked for many weeks about what might be next. Thanks be to God, I was offered scholarships at two institutions, one in Pittsburgh and the other one in D.C. We had to weigh not only the merits of each program, but also the cost of living and the likelihood of Sue's finding good work. I felt she should have the primary input—she made the decision to follow me to Atlanta, at the risk of her career, and she was subjected to my choice of living arrangements for the past year. Now she is moving again because of my education, and it was the very least I could do to listen to what she thought about where we should live. For her, the decision was not that complicated; she was uneasy about how expensive life would be in D.C. and thought that it was more likely to gain the supervision she'd need living just across the Pennsylvania border from her graduate school in Ohio. Yet I still wrestled with the decision—what if my potential employers considered the other program better or more prestigious? What if being away from the coast, and the many colleges and universities along the eastern seaboard, handicapped my opportunities to land a good teaching position? On the other hand, though, I wondered what might happen if I had to work part-time just to afford living there. I can't imagine not finishing the degree.

In the end, we decided on Duquesne University in Pittsburgh. It is the right decision, and we made it the right way. I am energized, ready to keep running. I've told her that I don't want a party or any fuss for my graduation from Emory; there are miles to go before we sleep. The major difference, of course, is that I no longer think of my career goal—that brilliant, sometimes blinding, conviction that I was made to be a professor—as a personal entitlement, but rather as a means toward our nascent family life. Every success I have, she shares; every disappointment affects both of us equally. Yes, I have often been moved by selfish motives—this will be her second move because of my graduate studies. This time, though, we have made the decision together. God bless her, she is willing to be the breadwinner for a while. I will be teaching in a few months, on my modest teaching assistant stipend, and that will help. But with two years of coursework in front of me, followed by a dissertation that will take who knows how long, the arrangement is not exactly temporary. I will work hard and quickly, knowing how desperately she longs to spend her energy in the beautiful role of a new mother.

8

WHEN WE HAD TO THROW AWAY THE SCRIPT (FALL, 1995)

I desperately want to believe that everything is fine, just fine, for it is written into the genes of all Irishmen that things are perfectly well until you are no longer able to hold onto a blade of grass to keep from flying off the face of the earth. And so my refrain has been "I'm sure it's nothing to worry about, hon, it's been only six (nine .. twelve . . .) months." And the months in question are those that have passed since we began actively seeking to bring a child into our world. Outwardly, I am at ease, while inside—the usually inaccessible part that stays buried as long as I'm doing something else—is beginning to be deeply, deeply worried.

The truth is that I have moved inexorably from carefree delight in the effort to concern to anguish. We began trying over a year ago, and I was both excited and, to be honest, nervous. Yes, I was halfway through coursework, meaning that we could plan for a baby's arrival after I finished, when I would be in a position to seek a full-time job in academia. But from my peers I knew that prospects were far from guaranteed, and that a future in bartending was not yet altogether out of the question. Yet I knew in my heart that she was right: it was time. We had entered marriage knowing that we wanted several children—we each have three siblings—and that the window for childbearing was going to be shortened by the demands of graduate school. At twenty-seven, she wanted to take positive steps toward realizing the dream she had nurtured and had invited me to share, for many years. But now we have reached the twelve-month mark with no success, meaning that now we've met the medical definition of infertility.

She was certain of it by the first month. Last September she was already beginning to panic; she had no doubt. I was flabbergasted: "How can you be so worried so early?" In retrospect, the answer is clear: she knows how her body works. I retained a somewhat passive-aggressive stance: no rush; more time to find a job next year; a baby will change everything; let's just enjoy the trying. Till now I have had the luxury of convincing myself that my theological vocation and my vocation as a husband were complementary. Now, with a very serious concern in our married life, I can think of my work only as a means to an end: I need a good job as soon as I can get it.

Early on in our marriage there was one occasion when I was sure that we were expecting. At that early stage the prospect of fatherhood was jarring. I loved the idea of having a child, recalling my pseudo-parenting role toward the brother and sister who are many years younger than me, but the lack of clarity about my professional future left me with grave concerns. I sweated out a week before learning that business was back to usual, relieved that no significant life change was yet in the offing. Now, however, things are different. She has carried the burden of supporting us for nearly three years, and it is time to move toward the next stage of our life. Yes, I am scared by the unknown, but I love and trust her enough to know that the decision to start really trying was the right one.

She grew concerned early mainly because we knew the signs. We had made the decision before we were married that our family planning would be based on careful observation of her fertility. For three years, we were wildly happy with it. Our communication about sex, and hope for our family, were an integral part of our married life, and the ritual checks of temperature and hormonal changes contributed to our hope. The desire for children suffused our daily life, even when we knew the time wasn't right. One day, we anticipated, we would arrive at the point when we could realize our hopes, and work together as carefully and thoughtfully toward achieving pregnancy as we once had in preparing for it.

Having reached that point over a year ago, we shared the disappointment that came a month later. Mine was more intellectual—of the "hmm, that wasn't supposed to happen" variety—whereas hers was deeply emotional. She was worried, and wanted to get tests done right away. I wanted to keep trying, knowing that the laws of biology are not always fully predictable. It was a measured, reasonable, logical response to the problem— but wholly inadequate. I completely missed the opportunity to comfort her, to enter into her distress, to sit with her in a place where she felt alone and afraid. I was living in the intellectual castle that was my abode; it was a neat place governed by the rules of conversation and reason, very unlike the emotional nest where she spent her days. For very much like a nest, it was comprised of the materials at hand: conversations with loved ones, personal experiences and observations, fears and hopes and dreams. Yes, I shared elements of that nest with her, but when I went off to my work in class or immersed myself in texts for research, I flew away to my castle and observed its elegant protocols with hardly a thought for anything else.

It was thus with no small amount of dismay that I received her suggestion in December that we consider adoption. "Whoa! That's a bit drastic, isn't it?" I said to her. "Sweetie, let's give it a little time."

Her face showed the weight of her thoughts. "I just don't want to be waiting for years before we even begin the process that will lead to a child. If we can think about both pregnancy and adoption at the same time, we can be certain that something will work."

I was skeptical. I had never even considered adopting a child, never known anyone I knew to be adopted. She could just as easily have suggested that I consider becoming pregnant myself. "It's been only three months, hon," I said. This was the first of several refrains that I would repeat in the succeeding months. The truth is that whereas I was scared of becoming a parent through pregnancy, I couldn't fathom becoming a parent through adoption.

She was hurting, and I could see it. "I saw an ad in the Pittsburgh Catholic newspaper about adoption from China. I'd like to learn more."

I must have looked like a deer in headlights. Adopting from China?

"I've felt drawn to adoption for a long time, especially from China. Can we just find out a little more information? There's a meeting at a local parish."

I can't even remember how I shot down the suggestion. I felt punched in the stomach by the idea, which seemed so far off my radar screen that I didn't even know how to interpret my response to it. I wasn't yet at the point of believing that there was any problem to be solved, and she was offering what seemed to me a life-changing solution. Implicitly, and probably explicitly, I indicated that I was not on board with this idea.

See Question 14 p. 141

She phoned the adoption agency to get more information, only to learn that the idea was a dead end. We were much too young, they had said; China specifies that both parents must be at least thirty-five at the time of adoption. Then there was the small matter of legal expenses, which mushroomed before me like an atomic bomb when I learned the details. I would have been perfectly content to put that idea to rest and move on with our life, were it not for her grief at this new information. Only when I witnessed her reaction to the news did something inside kick in. At some level she had already set her heart on this idea, and I hadn't taken the time to find out why.

The months since then have been focused on figuring out the medical picture. Somewhere between December and now I have come to agree that we have to get the testing done. In humility I have realized that she was right all along, that something is wrong, that we must spend our energy exploring all the information and praying that we make wise decisions, because clearly the easy way that seems so available to our friends, Hollywood bimbos, and irresponsible teenagers is unavailable to us. We have already suffered through the first Mother's Day—she left church sobbing midway through Mass. Now we must begin the process of beating whatever is keeping us from pregnancy.

The first wound is laying bare what ought to be hidden and treasured in secret. We had to put our sex life under the bright fluorescent lights of the clinic, an object of study and of trial and error. Early in our relationship sex was lyrical, symphonic; now it is like tuning a piano. It was the luxurious textures of a Van Gogh or the sensuous lines of a Rubens; now it is something like paint-by-numbers. We have had to pay attention to the results of various tests, wait from month to disappointing month, and wring our hands at the complete lack of control that we now feel.

The second wound, though, is much deeper. From very early in our relationship we understood that our friendship was rooted in a shared spirituality, a shared sense that our roots were sunk deep into holy ground, and that we were reaching in the same direction toward a God whose very presence among us was an act of love. It was not long, therefore, before we began to ask the bald question: "Why is God denying us the gift of children?" For her, the question emerged as another "crying out" like I had recalled when I proposed to her. She knew the biblical stories: Sarah, blessed with child in her old age; Hannah, whose prayer to God for a son was answered; Mary, graced by God to bear in her flesh the very presence of God among us. Childbearing was the sign of God's covenant, promise, trust; infertility was a withholding of the gift.

Both of us have degrees in theology and can understand the cultural and literary contexts of the biblical texts. We don't hold to the naïve belief that our experience of infertility is a sign of divine disfavor, and yet on a very basic level it is easy to understand why ancient peoples could perceive the inability to bear children as a curse or a punishment. This deficiency hurts—it hurts our self-understanding as a couple, and it hurts each of us individually in different ways.

For her, the hurt is in the way that it has made her body into an enemy. Our task has been to understand what it is doing, because it is not behaving the way we want it to. She can no longer retain the common, carefree, unreflective sense of self of those who have never experienced sickness, for the very skin through which she lives and moves in the world has rebelled against her will.

My hurt is a secondary hurt: I hurt because I know how much this is hurting her. I want to be able to tell her that I love her, that I am here for her, that I will stick with her no matter what happens, that no sickness can change the fact that I have chosen my life with her for better or worse. And yet while I do say these things to her constantly—for the reminders of our frustrations are constant—I know that there is nothing I can do, nothing I can say that can take away her pain. My hurt, therefore, is at my utter powerlessness, my inability to change what is happening to us.

Still, there is grace in the struggle. As much as our sex life has become for us an object of careful planning, it is nonetheless a consolation, a sign that we are in the midst of this struggle together. Yes, perhaps it has sometimes become less artful and more clinical, but in spite of this fact, there is still the most basic affirmation that this dimension of our life together is one that we waited for, treasured, and will always appreciate.

We have moved a long way from the sexual script that I remember in my early years in college. Today I am pulled in different directions: the desire to comfort her in her pain, the desire to cooperate with her in the process of diagnosis and prognosis; the desire to let her know that I will walk with her on this new phase of our pilgrimage, regardless of the still-unknown destination. Oddly, I find myself thankful for the intricacies of my body in ways that would have seemed strange when I was young. Then, it could be an unruly creature, hormones rushing at sometimes the slightest suggestion of desire. Now my sex life is governed by rules I consider sacred; they constitute the rhyme and meter of the poetry that has unfolded over these three years.

Under our present circumstances, there is a bodily wisdom that unfolds of its own accord, regardless of external stressors. Do the medical signs indicate that we must plan another attempt, or two, or three in coming days? I know this body, with its bundled software, will not be distracted from its role. I will attend to her, and let my body speak its own language.

See
Question
15
p. 141

9

WHEN WE FINALLY ARRIVED AT THE SAME PLACE (SUMMER, 1998)

The stress of recent days, months, and years has left us desperate for a place of calm, a place where we might pause long enough to see the direction in which we have been running full tilt. Our stay here will not be long, but even within the first hour of our arrival in Taizé I felt as though a minute here was worth at least two or three in most other parts of the world. I wish Sue could share my feelings, but the truth is that being in an atmosphere of prayer and silence is about the last place she wants to be right now.

God knows that we are looking for anything that might take our minds off the bad news we received a couple of days ago, just before boarding the plane for our post-dissertation European excursion. It seems that surgery and fertility treatments have not produced the desired outcome; we've hit another brick wall. What we had planned as a getaway to celebrate the conclusion of my graduate studies now feels like a retreat, to tend each other's wounds and struggle to find some way to move on with our lives. I who tend to crave islands of silence find this place refreshing. But what she needs right now is not more time to reflect but some distraction from the burden she's been carrying.

We are here through both planning and happenstance. I've known about this place since my Oxford days, having sometimes prayed with other students using Taizé chant in St. Mary's Church. The story of this place is fascinating: an ecumenical community founded in the wake of World War II for the sake of promoting peace, using the liturgical and devotional traditions of monasticism. I was too hyperactive to take in this place the last time I was in France but am glad to have the chance now. The opportunity presented itself when my friend Maleita invited us to meet here, so we'll spend a little time before heading to Italy together. Under different circumstances, I would love to stay and gather my thoughts for a longer while.

> *Wait for the Lord*
> *His day is near.*
> *Wait for the Lord*
> *Be strong, take heart.*

The words of the chant have been resounding in my brain all night. The open-air church was packed to the gills with young pilgrims from four continents, all breathing forth the words in slow unison. I can't say how long we sang these words, but the constant repetition impressed their urgency upon me, each refrain another drop of water soaking the sponge of my heart. These many months have been agonizing, hope after hope getting dashed against the rocks of pure biological futility. There is a violence to hope, for its constant reemergence is like tearing a bandage and reopening an old wound. Perhaps this surgery will help; perhaps this drug. Hope rises, hope falls and spills on the carpet, hope dies and is reborn again like a noxious weed. I have often wondered whether the finality of a clear prognosis would be easier: "Stop trying, it's impossible." As it is, we are offered glimmers, shards of hope that demand from us new expenditures of emotional and physical energy, and our tanks are all but empty.

> *Wait for the Lord*
> *His day is near.*
> *Wait for the Lord*
> *Be strong, take heart.*

To say that I have raged against God sounds trite. What I have experienced over the past three years has moved from denial to worry, to concern, to fear, to anger, to betrayal, to ever-deepening circles of futility. Now both Sue and I cry out to God, distracted only by the usual daily concerns of work and the inevitability of death and taxes.

We have had some respite in my professional progress and in her professional stability. She has been working in the counseling center of a small college for two years; it's a good position for her and has enabled me to write my dissertation quickly. I was hired last year as a professor at another small college, far enough into the writing that I was able to defend and earn the degree last month. We are now in a position to pay our bills, even as we wonder how we might grow our family.

It's becoming less and less likely that a pregnancy is in our future. We've seen specialists, we've tried the fertility drugs, but nothing is working. We've talked about the possibility of in vitro fertilization. But more and more we feel we are becoming subjected to a kind of reproductive technology machine that is playing on our desire to become parents. Neither of us wants to go down that road, in large part because we could never choose to selectively abort viable embryos.

See Question 16 p. 142

What we're beginning to realize in this process is that if we are going to undertake an emotional process at great expense, we have to be certain that it will ultimately lead us to a child. And so now the prospect of adoption seems more like something we need to take seriously. Or, I should say, it's something that *I* am praying about—hard—because it still seems be a very hard road, particularly because I have no idea how we can pay the legal fees. I feel, though, that I've committed myself to taking it, because I see now that she has been walking toward this road for some time now.

She has talked about it from time to time, gently introducing the idea into conversations. "Did you know that Gerald Ford was adopted?" or "Did you see that story about the Dave Thomas Foundation, which helps place kids in adoptive families?" A part of me has wanted to keep the subject at bay, but since last autumn I'm committing myself to praying about it. I suppose I could have taken a hard line, strong-armed our conversations: "We're not about to raise somebody else's child!" But I cannot utter that sentiment, no matter how often it lingers in the back of my mind. It wouldn't be the best me talking, the me that she deserves. And with that part of me shut up, what is left is the part that still wonders how to anticipate what's next.

It was in October when I came to understand a little better how this story will unfold. We had just moved into our new apartment in Indiana, Pennsylvania, a town halfway between our respective colleges. We were able to ride the rush of my new job for a couple of months in the summer and early fall; we were both making money and enjoying the stability that had eluded us since—well, always. But with that newfound stability came the inevitable question: when, then, can we move onto the next stage of our lives? What decisions do we make—to keep trying fertility treatments? What if they don't work? It was decision time, courage time.

"We need to talk," she said one day. I was in the second bedroom—my office, at least for now. Her tone was serious, and I knew that we had to sit down and suspend the rest of life for a while. "I'm thirty and I'm scared that we don't have any idea how we'll ever have children, and I need to know what you are thinking about all this."

I breathed deeply. How could I convey to her what I had been thinking about, feeling—when I could barely acknowledge it myself?

"I know, sweetie, I know. It's been hard on me too. I know it's been harder on you—you've had the surgery, you've taken the drugs, you've experienced the heartache in your own body. I know that, but I need you to understand that this has been very hard on me too."

I had struck the right chord. Her eyes were already misty as I held her hand. Her breath was short and it was clear that she was trying to keep from falling into sobs. "I needed to hear that," she said, and breathed out slowly, choosing her words carefully. "I need to know that you feel the same way I do." She paused and looked down at my hand holding hers, then looked at me, her eyes summoning mine. "I know you want to be optimistic and always look for hope, but now I need to know that you feel the same urgency I do, because things are not okay."

She was right; in our relationship I am the perpetual optimist, the one who will hold off acknowledging that things are bad until it is absolutely necessary. I was the one who didn't see the need for treatment right away; I was the one who said let's not jump to conclusions; I was the one who thought that rushing into an adoption was rash. In short, I was the one who was wrong on all counts.

"I know," I said, looking away, understanding that throughout this whole process it was she who was leading us, and I who was slowing us down. "I know, hon, and now I realize that you've been right, and I'm so sorry if I've not been there for you."

She was crying. Not much is harder for me to witness than her tears. I knew she was hurting deeply, and that there was little that I could do about it.

"I want to adopt a baby girl from China, and I need to know if you are ready to make a decision about this." Her eyes were plaintive, but her voice was decisive. It was clear that she was speaking from the soft and vulnerable place in her heart that even we, who are so forthright about our feelings for each other, seldom visit.

My answer came without hesitation. "I'm not ready now, but I will be."

Søren Kierkegaard wrote of faith as a leap into an unknown; this was what I was feeling. It was love for her that moved me to this act of trust in her judgment, even though I felt scared and unsure of what to anticipate. I was promising that even though I could not at that moment understand how our lives would change, how adoption might affect our relationship, our dreams for a family, our finances—I would give all my energy to the kind of conversion process that such a decision necessitated. What was I promising? I simply didn't know, and that unnerved me.

See Question 17 p. 142

During our wedding we had pronounced vows to love each other no matter what. We entered our life together with eyes wide open; it would not always be easy. Yet at this moment I recalled something that the priest celebrant at our wedding had said. Father Mark was a friend of ours—in fact, he had been my high school religion teacher, and we had reconnected during his graduate studies in Boston. He knew us well, and his line hit the mark exactly: "You enter marriage imagining you'll make sacrifices, and you end up making sacrifices you could never imagine." How right he was. At this moment, promising Sue that I would give my life over to the process of conversion, the process of coming to see myself not as the father of a Claire or Brendan, but rather of a Xiaoyi or a Liwei—it was like agreeing to travel blindfolded. Perhaps it was because I had internalized the need to take care of my family, and charted in my imagination the steps necessary to secure our well-being. But what was clear to me was that I needed to let go of what I had imagined, and simply trust that she was right, and that in this trust I would be listening in some way to God's own voice.

But something else became clear to me during this conversation. Sue's desire to adopt was not temporary. Yes, it was clear that the process of dealing with this deep hurt in our lives exposed corners of our hearts that might otherwise have remained buried under the veneer of satisfaction: a home, an enjoyable sex life, an easy route to babies and diversions and friends and the American Dream. Yet what I found in that exposed place in her heart was something altogether unexpected and yet very, very powerful: a desire to embrace a child whose need for a mother was as deep and lasting as her need for a child to love. Could such a desire be germinating in my own heart, buried (no doubt) under even thicker strata of defenses? To my surprise, I find myself beginning to pray that the seed has found fertile ground.

Part of what has made this prayer begin to emerge over the past few months is the fact that I am no longer thinking about adoption abstractly, as a kind of calculus of pros and cons about how easy or difficult raising an adopted child might be. Instead, I think about how she speaks about wanting to adopt, about wanting to mother a child. Last May, when we traveled together to a professional conference in St. Louis, she and a friend went exploring Union Station. She related to me how she came across a *St. Louis Magazine* story about adopting from China—it was a lovely story about a little girl named Jade. The story moved her, even as it caused her consternation, knowing as she did that the option to adopt from China was not available to us, at least in the short term. Later that day, though, while perusing the shops, she happened across a family with a little three-year-old girl adopted from China. She related to me what she felt: a deep sense of longing to go to China, even the conviction that her daughter was there.

At the time, I was both moved and troubled by her story; I simply could not see an international adoption as something we could afford, and so I felt helpless. But on some level I was happy to see the joy in her eyes even telling the story.

That conference was just over a month ago, not long before our latest heartbreak. The scales are tipping: on one side is the weight of medical evidence; on the other is the still-vague hope for adoption. I know where the experiences of the one side have brought us: anger, helplessness, and frustration. But I don't yet know where the other side leads.

Wait for the Lord
His day is near.
Wait for the Lord
Be strong, take heart.

And so here we are, amidst a world of young people who have left home to travel as pilgrims to this place of refreshment, of living water, to pray in earnest to know the will of a living God. Some are in the midst of discerning vocations, perhaps to marriage or to religious life, to a new profession or relationship. Others have left places where there is war or political turmoil, or broken families, or communities ripped asunder by drugs or the ravages of AIDS, to sit for a while in a place of peace, a place of prayer. She and I have left our comfortable home in a quiet part of the world, yet still driven to listen carefully to God's echoed whispers, in the hope that what we do might be a salve to our pain and perhaps even a good for the world we inhabit. I cannot imagine her—God's beloved, and mine—living without being a mother to a child. I'm beginning to believe now that our challenge is first to learn where the child lives.

10

How Far Thirty Is from Twenty (October, 2000)

I have heard friends complain about turning thirty, because it's supposed to represent a point beyond which their youth begins to slip into the past, and dreaded middle age looms large like a sickness. In contrast, I've been looking forward to turning thirty for many months now; for Sue and me it represents the beginning of the next stage of our pilgrimage—the stage that leads, at long last, to parenthood by way of China. Not long ago, this idea had faded from our minds for the simple reason that it seemed both legally and financially impossible. But now—amazingly—those hurdles no longer exist. Our paperwork is sitting in a bureaucrat's office in Beijing. I am learning to speak Mandarin. In my wallet is a photo of a wide-eyed, six-month-old little girl who will be my daughter, and within a couple of months I will meet her for the first time.

Our weekend trip from western Pennsylvania back to Boston represents a rite of passage, a look backwards and a look forward. I came to race in the Head of the Charles Regatta yesterday, a race that at one time meant everything to me. Now, because of turning thirty, I fall into the race's Masters Division. I'm looking back at the past seven years of our married life, and before that at the previous five years of my student life. I am not the same person that last raced here nine years ago as a senior in college. Back then, I looked forward to growing my professional career and marrying a wonderful woman; I carried optimism like an easy shoulder sack. When I raced, it was because I loved the excitement of competition, of putting hard work to the test and feeling the thrill of performance, ever to excel. Today, however, that attitude is only a memory that lurks like a stowaway. Perhaps there is a part of me that wanted to recapture something of old glory; but this race was also a celebration of what is to come. I raced because on some level I needed to focus on something that gave me joy, something that allowed me to give thanks for who I was created to be, and not constantly lament what had been missing from our life. For my entire adult life, I have loved the feeling of physical fitness, of commitment and discipline and working toward a goal. This race was for me a statement about perseverance, even amidst the problems Sue and I have had to face.

When we began our adoption paperwork about two years ago, I knew that I wanted to do this race one last time before the demands of parenthood and work made it impossible. Dealing with infertility all these years has been difficult enough, and the prospect of placing our lives in the hands of others—a host of unseen agents, from birth parents on the other side of the world, to government bureaucrats on two continents, to lawyers and social workers—felt intensely stressful. I wanted the focus of something familiar, some kind of struggle that depended primarily on my own hard work and training. When I broached the subject with her, she understood immediately, God bless her.

Once upon a time I would have entered this competition having trained hard for the previous six months. As a collegiate rower my work ethic was second to none; as the men's captain during my senior year at Boston College, I prided myself on leading by example. I did double workouts during much of the year, trained on my own over the summer—back then I believed that success was a matter of insuring that there was absolutely no room for regret. Success had to do with competence and preparation.

That was nine years ago. Today, I have new priorities, new concerns, and new expenditures of time and mental energy. I have gotten out on the water as often as I could, but often made the decision to head home to be with Sue on otherwise lonely evenings. I have gotten on the rowing machine, but wince to see the time I am able to pull these days. It is respectable, I suppose, but far slower than the times I pulled when I was at peak form. I came to this race terrified that this would be my first "DFL." We used to joke about those sorry competitors who just didn't belong: "DFL" was the name we gave them, where "D" stood for "dead" and "L" stood for "last."

I knew upon entering this race that many of those I would be racing were men who had stayed competitive over the years. In rowing, many of the best are those who have matured in the sport. Many Olympians are in their thirties, and some have even hit forty. So age was no excuse for me. And as a true lightweight I knew that I would be at a disadvantage, since there are no weight divisions at the Masters level in the Head of the Charles. Still, it was important to mark this passage of years with this race that meant so much to me as a student. It was the race of all races, the event that drew a quarter of a million people to the banks of the river in Boston, a pageant to an ancient and still tradition-laden sport that only a few choose to undertake as amateurs. It was Oxford and Cambridge, Harvard and Yale, John Kelly (Princess Grace's father) and more recently, the ageless British oarsman

Steven Redgrave, who won his fifth Olympic gold medal in Sydney. Also, it was the poetry of mornings on a glassy river.

But for me, the race was also just simply an expression of joy. I am happy to be thirty, happy to be preparing to welcome a child into our home, happy to have been sharing a struggle with a beautiful woman, and happy to be capable of feeling in my own body the great good of flowing blood and straining muscle, with Virgil's lines echoing in my mind.

> *All take their seats, and wait the sounding sign:*
> *They gripe their oars; and ev'ry panting breast*
> *Is rais'd by turns with hope, by turns with fear depress'd.*

My years of competitive rowing, both in Boston and Oxford, were some of the best of my life. I felt alive, able to take on any struggle. I suppose that this year I wanted to recapture some of that. But at the same time it was nice to realize that I no longer cling to racing as the place where my life struggles play out. This race was more of a parable, similar to the many stories of hope that unfold at every Boston Marathon. Here are the people racing to raise money for cancer research; there are the people racing in memory of a loved one, or in celebration of quitting smoking, or in hope for a cure for any number of diseases. For me, the race was about moving beyond the years of defeat and hardship, heartbreak and hopelessness, and committing myself to looking forward to adoption. I had promised Sue more than two years ago that I would one day be ready, and that day has come.

See Question 18 p. 142

It has come with difficulty. After the great letdown preceding our trip to Europe we came home resolved to work with the doctors for a few more months to see if anything might help. By

August it was clear that we had to pursue all possible options, including more drugs and surgery by a specialist out of state.

Having a counseling background herself, Sue was wise enough to begin seeing a counselor before it became a crucial necessity. I stretched my capacity to comfort her in her pain but at the same time was coming to name and acknowledge my own. Sue recognized this and understood that she needed someone besides me to help her process the many emotions she had to withstand daily. I was relieved; although I was doing everything I could, before long I realized that I could help her only so much. I simply wasn't equipped emotionally to understand all that she was going through. It was one of those times when I had to face my limitations, even in this great love relationship. It hurt me too much to talk with her at great length about how much she was hurting.

See
Question
19
p. 143

"You end up making sacrifices you could never expect." Father Mark's prescient words, while difficult, were in some way a consolation. This process has stretched me even more than I could have imagined, to the point where I am not only ready but openly excited about the life that awaits us. As a result, I have come to a certain humility about my feelings at any given moment, knowing that love might move me to change the way I feel. I have come to understand my limits, too—I am not perfect, least of all in the complex vocabulary of the emotional life in which Sue is utterly fluent. I can love her with my broad paintbrush, but allow those with much finer bristles to minister to her in ways that address those points which I strain to understand even today.

It was during the counseling process that Sue began to more clearly identify her desire to adopt. Specifically, she felt hung up on our not qualifying to adopt from China, and she developed a conviction that her daughter was there. More and more of her sessions dealt with the sense of loss that Chinese adoption represented, even as the medical concerns about failure to conceive slowly dropped into the background.

Amidst these counseling sessions we received the news that we still were unable to conceive. The news was hard, but not earth-shattering; much of our world had already crumbled. It was more like the last air going out of a slowly leaking balloon, a whimper rather than a bang. We would never be parents through pregnancy.

It would be wrong to say this news wasn't devastating. Over the coming months, and even years, we would continue to process the fact that we would never experience what so many of our friends would experience. Yet at the same time, I think both of us realized that it was time to turn our full attention to adoption, to look ahead to the obvious next choice rather than dwell on the difficulty of the one that was closed off to us.

Now that I think back on that transition of a couple years ago, I wonder why it didn't come sooner. There is a powerful script that moves people from marriage into childbearing, and my own tenacious clinging to the hope of pregnancy was rooted in the desire to stick to the script. As I understood it then, the script required strength and perseverance on my part—a willingness to overcome any obstacle in order to make it to the desired outcome—a young Claire or Brendan. My years of physical training had taught me that any goal is worth every possible effort; this struggle was but the latest version of that basic lesson.

We held on to that script—I more than she, perhaps because she is more in tune with the wisdom of her emotions. As the data of our lives made the script less and less relevant, I was left with the need to find another plotline. And when we finally had to toss out the script altogether, I discovered that she had been developing a perfectly good alternate all along.

See Question 20 p. 144

People have asked me in recent months whether adopting feels like a second-best option. I answer them honestly: at first, it did. For the first few years when we were dealing with infertility, adoption did represent for me a failure to stay with the struggle and see it to its completion. Now I see how self-centered that attitude was; it was about what I was feeling, what my desires focused on. I wanted her to be happy; I wanted a nice, happy life with a new baby and grandparents cooing over how the baby had her eyes and my hair. I wanted to stick to the script; it seemed like a good script. And while I was trying to see it through, it did seem as though tossing away the script was like quitting or copping out.

Now, though, I've come to see things differently. I can't say when or how it happened, but I can see the difference. In large part, it is due to the fact that Sue's desire to adopt has always been there; the collapse of the script just made it all the more obvious. For me, letting go of the script has given me the chance to question what it is that I've really wanted all along. Yes, I want to make her happy. But I also want us to be looking out toward the world, instead of gazing narcissistically at each other all the time. What I want is not primarily to pass along our genes (what's so great about them, anyway?), but rather to share with her the experience of raising a child.

That, in a nutshell, was the conversion process. It has involved a lot of letting go—for me, releasing the experience of seeing her give birth and nurse our baby. But it has also involved a good deal of surprise and anticipation, especially around the excitement of welcoming a child into our lives for the first time, of reaching out across cultures to create a family.

At first, we were uncertain on so many fronts. How would we adopt? How would we pay for it? What were the steps people had to take? Would we qualify? Would people be judging us? What if they didn't think we were capable? We had visions of having to persuade young birth mothers to choose us over any number of others, and it was frightening to imagine subjecting ourselves to even more emotional roller coaster rides. It was primarily because of that fear that we began thinking seriously about international adoption, which seemed less likely to unbalance the fragile state we felt ourselves in.

Still, there were the dual concerns of eligibility and financing. International adoption appeared to be the right idea, and Sue clung to the hope that somehow we would find our way to China. Secretly I was unsure whether we could make it happen.

The first ray of sunshine came almost exactly two years ago, in an ad that she saw in a local paper. An adoption agency reported that China had modified its age requirement, and that parents who were over thirty now qualified for adopting baby girls. We went to the meeting in a nearby church and listened to the stories of two families who had recently adopted from China. Their new daughters were there, climbing playfully around their mothers' laps. Very quickly I could see in Sue's face the conviction that we would be heading to China before long. I had been praying and praying for clarity, for wisdom, for good decision making, for a generous heart; the answer to my prayer was the unequivocal clarity that emerged in her eyes after that meeting.

"I think I want to name her Grace," she said.

I looked at her with curiosity. "After the social worker?" I was referring to the native-born Chinese woman who, with her brother working in China, spearheaded the Chinese adoption process for the agency.

"No, no," she said, smiling. "I just think it's a beautiful name."

"I like it too. Grayce was my grandmother's name." I pictured us as parents of a little Grace, and the image made me smile. "I also like it because it's clear to me that this child will be exactly that for us—a grace, a gift, a manifestation of God's love for us all through this whole process. You've known it all along—ever since we started trying—that we'd be adopting from China. You've been listening. You've known that's where we'd find our daughter. Now I just wish I'd listened better, sooner.

"Besides," I continued, "We can't have a Chinese girl stuck with a name like 'Claire Muldoon'—it'll just confuse people."

She was laughing, and I laughed too. "For God's sake," I said, "it's confusing enough that she'll be a Muldoon—people will expect a step dancer with curly red locks. Let's at least call her something that tones down the whole ethnic thing."

From that moment on, it was clear that our married life was about developing the momentum that would one day bring us to China. I had no idea how we'd pay the fees. I had no idea what sort of preparations we would need to undertake, but I saw that some day we would bring a daughter home from a place which, once upon a time, I could not even imagine being such a central part of my world. What felt exhilarating about this new resolve was that it gave us a shared focus, a shared sense of striving for something that would stretch us and shape us in ways that we could not predict. In one sense, it felt like training: it was a distant goal that required a great deal of work, and so presented me with a new focus. There were still many hurdles to overcome, but at least now we were no longer mired in the entropy of raised and dashed hopes.

Our immediate concerns were threefold. First, we had to start thinking hard about how to finance this adventure. Second, we had to see through the medical treatments Sue was undergoing, those that emerged as necessary responses to the tests over recent years. Third, we had to begin the long, byzantine process of gathering papers and legal documents in order to prepare the dossier that one day would be sent to the Chinese government. Months and even years began to stretch out before us; we knew there would still be mountains to climb before we could settle into ordinary family life.

I recalled a memory of our young relationship, perhaps even weeks old. I'd shared with her an un-extraordinary picture that had become for me a distinct longing: I imagined lounging on a couch watching a movie together late at night. That's it. I shared how much I wanted the feeling of being at home with her, of savoring the simple pleasure of resting in the knowledge that when I awoke, she would be there. Thinking ahead to adoption, I felt a similar longing: I envisioned an ordinary Friday night at home, making homemade pizza (which we did nearly every Friday) and enjoying the company of kids settling in to watch a cartoon movie. Again, it was the feeling of at-homeness that I desired, of being shelter to each other. Who is the child who will fill in the picture? What challenges must we face before that picture is a reality?

The most pressing issue was obtaining the funds we would have to present up front. Early in the process we learned about the tax credit, the money we'd be getting back the year following the adoption. But we still had to find cash, and so we began investigating ideas. Home equity loan? Nope, we rent. Company with generous adoption reimbursement policy? Nope, not while working for small colleges. Personal loan from the bank? Not with our almost complete lack of assets. What about grants or adoption loans? No, and no. I was getting worried that the plan would stall before we made any progress.

We were committed nonetheless, and began talking about our hopes with friends and relatives. Sue came alive as she talked about going to China; she was excited, yet serious. Just seeing her talk this way made me happy and increased my resolve. Maybe I could find a summer job when the academic year was over, or maybe I could make some money off my writing. What was changing in my approach to the whole situation was that my heart was leading, and my head was trying its best to find solutions. I trusted Sue completely; I trusted her intuitions, her passions, her drive to move us toward the place where she was certain her daughter was. And I found myself becoming more and more excited too.

At Thanksgiving, one of my relatives offered us the money to pay for the adoption fees. We could not believe it; we cried with joy and decided to get our paperwork started as soon as we completed the medical treatments following the turn of the new year. This was an unexpected gift from an unexpected source; neither of us comes from wealth, and so the gift of that money was an outpouring of great generosity from someone who did not have a lot of money to throw around. It freed us to start thinking about ourselves as parents, charged with the task of bringing our daughter home.

The out-of-state treatments were the last gasp of the life we'd been leading for the previous several years, of attending to a diagnosis that brought pain, and yet paradoxically grew in us a tenderness and attentiveness dedicated to working through the pain together. My efforts at being present to her were aided by the anticipation that all this would soon be over and that soon we would be turning our attention to the adoption process. I began imagining us as the parents of a Chinese baby girl; I began imagining her as a mother. And that image—of her holding our baby—melted any lingering doubts. There was a moment when she was lying down, about to see the doctor, stressed and ready to go home. Thinking about this image of her, I began massaging her face with the tips of my fingers, just seeking to calm her nerves and make her feel comfortable. For several minutes, I just lightly grazed her skin and contemplated this image, feeling incredibly thankful that now we were able to put behind us the stresses of the previous several years. Here was my beloved, the one with whom I had fallen in love, and with whom I was still falling in love, who had suffered much and who had grown tired. Here was I, similarly wearied by the work of these years, yet still in a position to comfort her and care for her. *Here we are,* I thought, calming the muscles in her face, *about to embark on something so entirely different from what we envisioned for ourselves five, six, seven, eight years ago, and yet this different thing is becoming for us both a source of great joy and anticipation.*

We began the paperwork in February, hoped to have it completed by spring, and hoped to travel the following spring, when she was thirty-two and I was a few months shy of thirty. We had learned from the agency that there was roughly a twelve- to fourteen-month wait time from when the dossier landed in China, and so our best hope was that we might travel in May the following year. In the back of our minds was the question of whether they'd hold us up until both of us were thirty; we hoped not. I was nervous—I really hated the idea that I might hold up the process because of being too young.

We collected the necessary documents from all over the Northeast: wedding license from Massachusetts; my birth certificate from Virginia; proper authorizations from the Chinese consulate in D.C., and state authentication in Pennsylvania. We spent spring break road-tripping from western Pennsylvania to D.C. to Harrisburg for the necessary signatures and notarizations. We spent countless hours organizing, making copies, double-checking, and finally sending all the documents to the agency by way of the most heavily insured, tracked-by-radar-and-satellite system known to humankind. The agency received our materials, sent them to the translators, and eventually sent them on to the China Center of Adoption Affairs.

Then we waited.

We didn't know how long the wait would be, and it was agonizing. We knew it would be at least ten or eleven months, and so initially the waiting wasn't much different from waiting for a pregnancy to come full term. Sue was ecstatic to finally be falling into nesting mode, and I was happy to see her in that role. I was only slowly beginning to really imagine what fatherhood was going to be like; it was still an abstraction for me. I saw my role primarily as attending to her—she seemed so much more aware of what needed to be done. We needed a crib, a stroller, clothes, bottles, bibs—the sheer volume of equipment was daunting. And we needed to learn what to expect; we attended sessions on international adoption that addressed health and developmental concerns, attachment issues, language issues, and so on. Our world became intensely focused on parsing the complexity of the task before us, for not only did we have the ordinary life change of a first baby, but also the added difficulty of understanding the particular challenges posed by both adoption and the differences of culture.

Sue was amazing. On some level she had already become a mother, for her life was now consumed by all things that affected her relationship to the little girl who was then only an idea in her mind. I could see that the years of struggle with fertility now were giving way to the most beautiful unfolding of a long-buried desire to adopt a child. The struggles to conceive were a distraction from this desire, which was now in full flower even before we met our daughter. I felt myself yearning for the moment when we would see her picture.

As May approached, we paid close attention to the news coming from the China Center of Adoption Affairs. We were part of a match group that would be receiving news together, and we hoped that it would come soon. The wait was becoming interminable.

I was the first recipient of the bad news that our dossier was being held up because of my age; it came while Sue was away at a professional conference in D.C. Frustration was nothing new to me; it was like the deadbeat roommate who shows up from time to time to make life miserable. This time, like on so many other occasions, I felt completely helpless. How can you argue about age? About the absurdity of making a thirty-two-year-old woman wait however many more months to meet her daughter because she's married to a kid of twenty-nine? About the fact that being married to me—rather than being single—is holding up her happiness?

It was a Friday; my classes were finished for the week, and so I got in the car and drove down to tell her. There would be no training that weekend.

We hurt some more, but we hurt together. This was no longer only her pain. . It was a hard weekend, but there was much grace in it. We realized that this was only a setback, a slowdown, not a dead end. We had more time to prepare (we rationalized), and we were still in this together. We decided to enjoy the weekend in a beautiful city instead of wallowing in the most recent frustration. I was proud of us.

May passed. June passed. July passed. We didn't know when to expect our news, but when August passed (and my thirtieth birthday, which we celebrated in grand style during the surprise party she threw), we began again to look with great expectations for the envelope that would have to arrive someday soon.

Meanwhile, I continued to train as well as I could. I needed the exertion just to calm the stress that tends to reside in my body. I found mornings on the water a source of great comfort, a kind of living recollection of a calmer time in my life. There is something hypnotic about rowing, about taking stroke after stroke in search of that Zen-like experience of blending in perfect harmony with the water. It provided a stirring and altogether welcome contrast to the rest of our anxious life and gave me something specific to turn my energies to.

In early September, my friend Anna offered me the use of her boat to race at the Head of the Charles. I had coached her a few years earlier, and we had sustained our friendship in the intervening years. She understood how much this race meant to me, and since she too was planning on racing there, she insisted that I use her boat for my event. I was very grateful, realizing with some amazement that I hadn't made any sort of previous plan about what boat I'd be using. So for the last few weeks before the event, we scheduled alternating times for us to take the boat out: she would go in the mornings, I in the evenings.

There have been very few moments in my life when I've experienced the kind of serendipity that I could call Providence. I prefer to speak softly about the way God works in the world. But the first evening I took Anna's boat onto the water was one of those providential moments, and it made me laugh out loud.

Here I was in the final weeks of preparation for the race, anticipating the arrival of a picture of my future daughter. Here I was, looking forward to a race that was for me a rite of passage, a celebration of the life that God had been shaping with me for the past thirty years and an anticipation of the new life that awaited us in the very near future. I was mindful of the many graces that had unfolded over the past decade that had brought us to this point, and spine-tinglingly mindful that our Grace was alive somewhere on the other side of the planet, unaware that her and our futures were soon to collide. Sometime after I put the boat in the water, and after I had gone to collect my blades, I stopped in my tracks, transfixed by the fact that I was about to row a boat that Anna had innocently given the name *Saving Grace*.

It was in that boat that I raced yesterday. Grace's picture stayed with me down the course; it arrived a few days ago, and we celebrated its arrival in grand style. She looks beautiful! She will be ten months old when we meet her, in six weeks or so. This all feels so real now—it was not hard to find inspiration for the race, for grace upon grace. It was a great race; I felt charged in a way I hadn't in a long time. The current members of the Boston College crew cheered me down the course—I wore the colors of my alma mater—as did a number of family members and old friends from the team.

I do miss the hard-core workouts I did when I was younger, and the feeling of coming into races confident that I had done everything humanly possible to make myself fast. For this race, I've not had that kind of single-minded commitment. I am still a young professor hoping to make my mark on the world. I have bills to pay, I hope we can buy a home some day, I hope that at some point my beloved can be a full-time mom, I hope that I might write something that will be useful to someone. I don't have three hours every day to get on the water, or lift weights, or run stairs. I came into this race knowing I am not the best but have done the best I could in this current life. Sue and I have chosen our priorities, and I'm happy.

And I did not finish last!

11

WHY WE JOURNEYED TO THE OTHER SIDE OF THE WORLD (DECEMBER, 2000)

I am falling in love. Even in spite of the many ways I have prepared for this experience, I am surprised and amazed at how it is happening. But the simple truth is that this child has captured my heart; I am smitten and out-of-control in love with her.

The only comparison I can draw is falling in love with Sue eleven years ago. I am not the master of my heart; it has been captured and drawn out of its comfortable resting place, stretched and bounced like a plaything. I can only marvel. For most of my life I have wanted to believe that I was in charge, that I could control the major decisions of my life with relative good judgment. These experiences of falling in love have made me appreciate how apt the phrase is: they have *felt* like falling, like being subjected to laws over which I exercise no control, but which exert their force upon me. Years ago, I could speak what I felt for Sue only with a firm resolve, because a part of me was terrified. This time, I am past the terror, and I've had the resolve for some time. Now I can simply enjoy the squeals of delight that erupt from Grace's ten-month-old mouth every time I swing her above my head or play peekaboo.

When we met her yesterday with the eleven other American families who were adopting from the same orphanage, we were more than a little nervous. Each family was called to meet their new daughter. Our turn was toward the end, after the large hotel meeting room was already filled with tears, wails, laughter, and many people trying mightily to get the right camera angle. We practically sprinted to meet the orphanage workers when our number was called; we saw our child across the room and recognized her from the picture we'd been clutching since we left for the airport. When she was placed in Sue's arms, her face contorted in a desperate expression of fear, and she could only utter a miserable half-cry, "umm-ma," over and over again through tears. I felt helpless to comfort her.

After a while her plaintive cries yielded to sleep, her small body exhausted at having traveled many miles from the only home she'd ever known to the big city and the strangers who were now holding her. My beautiful wife, the mother of my child, took her back to our room while I stayed behind to manage the paperwork that needed immediate attention.

When I rejoined them an hour and half later, Grace had awakened and was taking food. She had calmed down and seemed fine; she was very hungry, which was a good sign. She likely hadn't had much to eat during the day, and the fact that she trusted us to feed her was important. We knew that the coming days were uncertain: we didn't know how she would react to us, to her new environment, to the food we'd brought. We were braced for struggle, and so this initial positive sign was a great relief to us. We ourselves were very tired, having arrived in China only a couple of days earlier, and still jet-lagged from the twelve-hour time difference.

This morning, though, was glorious, one of those days I'll never forget. We awoke not long before Grace and simply stared at her beautiful, beautiful face while she slept. The photo did not do her justice: it was cold and two-dimensional, while in reality her features were delicate and radiant. Her cheeks held a healthy, ruddy glow; her eyes were classic Han; her face was heart-shaped and her lips a deep red. When she awoke, she looked around the room somewhat quizzically before focusing on the sight of the two of us. At that moment, her expression changed: she began *beaming* "I'm so happy to see you again!" we imagined her saying, and fell into spontaneous laughter. I picked her up and brought her atop the bed, where the three of us spent a long time simply playing and staring at each other with joy.

Today we'll have some time to explore this city, the capital of Anhui Province. Grace was born south of here, in the city of Anqing on the banks of the Yangtze River, but was brought to the capital city so that we could jump through the necessary local bureaucratic hoops.

I can't wait to learn about this place, so foreign and yet now so much a part of our family story. Ever since we crawled wearily off the plane in Hong Kong and began to take in where we were, my mind has been inhaling information. I wish I'd begun learning to speak Mandarin sooner. I want to know what people think about, how they look at the world, what they hope for—anything to help me understand the world that our new daughter has come from. From Hong Kong we took a bus ride into mainland China, passing through the checkpoint at the border. The ride to Guangzhou gave me ample time to look out the window and imagine and think about what was happening. Here we were, not unlike Connecticut Yankees in

King Arthur's Court, just trying to make sense of the fact that our Irish Catholic families would now have a Chinese side too. How does one become Chinese? Is there some kind of conversion process or ritual celebration? In truth, though, I feel that a part of me has already begun thinking of our family as half Chinese and that we have much to learn in order to understand how to honor that part of us.

We have come a long, long way. The irony that the pilgrimage of our relationship has brought us to the other side of the earth—the longest possible journey—is not lost on either of us. It began as a desire to know one another, to be present to each other, to spend time discovering ourselves in conversation with the other. Our early relationship began as a seed of friendship, which germinated in attraction and flowered into a transcontinental romance. But that was only the first phase of this pilgrimage, a phase that strengthened our mutual resolve that ours would be a magnificent love affair. In retrospect, it's clear that we needed that kind of resolve. Recalling the spring of my sophomore year in college, when I stayed awake nights thinking about her, I can see that there was a deep heart-wisdom, a knowledge that my restless heart was reaching out to her as one whose presence would bring me peace. I have learned to trust that wisdom in light of the past few years, when ordinary left-brain thinking would have kept me from trusting Sue's intuitions.

See Question 21 p. 144

I didn't always trust well. Early on, I was afraid of the directions that our desire for children was taking us; I anticipated the suffering they might entail. I'm not always the master of my own desires; sometimes they're unruly, and sometimes they originate in pain or bias. But one great grace of married life is that shared desires tend to purify and even marginalize more selfish ones. I have learned to test my desires by understanding hers, mindful that those we share more often point us in the direction of what will make our lives happy.

We have traveled a long way in our pilgrimage, only to arrive at this point, where we begin an entirely new one. Grace is still a baby; what will our lives be like when she begins to articulate what she feels, what she hopes for? How will we be stretched to love her in the ways that she needs, especially considering the challenges particular to being an Irish and Chinese family? One thing is clear now: I'm excited at the road ahead. I am eager to learn about her, but also to get to know her and what she will bring into our lives.

I look at Sue's face while she holds Grace in her arms, and my heart is full. The one I love has found her heart's desire, the child who will receive what Sue has been yearning for so long to give. There's a paradox in finding one's joy in the joy of another, something that strikes me as uniquely human. Perhaps this is what the biblical writer meant when describing human beings as created in God's image. For while it's true that we desire to be desired by the one we desire, it's also true that we desire to see a beloved's fulfillment of desire, even if the object of desire is a small child from a country a world away.

For many years now I have sought to love this woman as she deserves to be loved, and I've come to realize that it's narrow to imagine that I alone could fulfill everything she seeks out of life. I, too, am realizing the depth of my own desire to father this child, to give of myself so that she might grow and learn and live an abundant life. I have been pulled outside myself into a world that is much grander. By God's mercy I have not been allowed to rest contently in the satisfaction of small desires. These people in my life have challenged me, have summoned from me new and great desires that urge me to press on in this pilgrimage, eager to know what lies around the next corner.

12

HOW I FELL IN LOVE
THREE TIMES
(SPRING, 2006)

It's a beautiful day. In the warm sunshine, the five of us have just passed through the front gates of Disneyland, listening to the speakers pour out a refrain that strikes me as perfectly scripted.

Welcome to our fam-i-ly time,
Welcome to our happy-to-be time . . .,

I am skipping several yards ahead of Sue and her mom, who at this moment are no doubt watching Grace, Katie, and me with tears in their eyes. They, who will sometimes get misty at a TV commercial, are for certain delighted to witness this scene: a dad skipping hand in hand, and hand in hand, with the daughters he absolutely loves. Grace has just turned six, and Katie is three and a half, and they are gorgeous. As a three-year-old, Grace came with us on our second trip to China to adopt Katie when she had just turned a year old. The trip helped Grace understand more exactly what this whole adoption thing is about. I think she gets it when I tell her that I have fallen in love exactly three times in my life, and that she was time number two.

Falling in love is dangerous and therefore thrilling, because it means that your happiness is irrevocably tied up in the life of another sovereign creature. It means that you relinquish any illusion of being capable of managing life, because its complications are multiplied by the very fact that you care deeply about everything that impinges on the lives of those you love. Today, anticipating some fun at a precious time in my young daughters' lives, I feel buoyed by the simple joy of knowing they are happy. I know that at other times we will face struggles, perhaps even very serious ones. The happy times may be multiplied, but so too the experiences of pain; there are simply more of both because of the number of travelers. Today I wish there was a bank in which we could save this experience, to draw upon it later, when I will say to them, "Remember what a beautiful day it was at Disneyland? And how we all felt so happy to be there together?" I will certainly remind them of this moment when they are having bad dreams or are unsure of whether the world can be a hospitable place.

See Question 22 p. 145

My daughters spent nearly the whole first year of their lives in an orphanage. We will never know what it was like there, but we will always feel it is our job to overwhelm them now with what we imagine they missed there: individual attention, constant touch, soft words at night, a sense of hope. We pray for their birth parents, whose choice to leave them with others must have been wrenching—their daughters are so beautiful, so full of life. I pray for their early caretakers, too, some of whom I met and spoke with enough to know that they really loved these girls. But most of all I pray for us, that we will make wise decisions for them until they gain the freedom to make wise decisions for themselves. I am already beginning to see the shoots of this freedom in Grace, who is growing into a lovely, sensitive, and deeply caring girl, the perfect *jiejie*, big sister. Not long before our second trip to China, her refrain was "When are we going to China to get my baby?" And once we were there, I could see her taking on the responsibility of helping young Katie feel safe with us. She was Katie's proof that we—the big-nosed, strange white people—were okay.

Not long before the trip, we shared the match picture of Katie with some friends who similarly had adopted two daughters from China. "Don't you just want to put some sparkle in those eyes?" one had remarked. I was reminded of that question when, early after our first meeting with her, Katie seemed reluctant to open up to us. It was Grace who helped her know that it was safe to do so, and over the subsequent months, even after a period in which Katie would not let me touch her, we saw a bright-eyed child emerge with a quick sense of humor.

My falling in love with Katie took place in stages. There was the first expectation that unfolded when we received the match picture; then the slow, methodical process of coming to under-stand how this child needed time to adjust to her new family and especially to me—likely the first man in her daily life. Gradually there were her hesitant efforts to allow me to sit with her, read to her, and finally hold her; and after awhile there were playtimes, piggyback rides, long nights holding her hand as she (slowly) went to sleep, and tender, peaceful snuggles watching a movie and eating homemade pizza. Even now I marvel at how far we've come in these two-and-a-half years; I love falling in love with her.

The journey to bring Katie home was very different from our trip nearly three years earlier with Grace. The adoption process seemed so much more manageable because this time we had a better idea of what to expect throughout. Much of the anxiety was gone; though with the longer wait time that had developed in the intervening years, we were no less eager to go when the time finally came. Perhaps the greatest difference was that whereas Sue had moved tectonic plates to make the first trip possible, I was in many ways the prime mover the second time. I found, after our first year with Grace, that it was inconceivable for her to not have a sister or brother and for us to raise only one child. I, who had been afraid of considering adoption at one time, was so enthralled by the experience that I couldn't imagine not repeating it. At one point I observed to a friend that I would feel great regret if we could not adopt again, even if pregnancy were possible. By that point, I'd grown in the conviction that adoption was part of our calling as a couple, because it represented the grace of transforming our suffering into a new joy shared with a child who had also suffered. At one time we had to let go of the hope of children; at one time an orphan has to let go of the hope of parents.

That experience of finding joy in the boundary-crossing act of welcoming a child into our lives has been transformative. It has changed my priorities, my hopes, my free time, and my sense of gratitude. And perhaps more than anything else, it has rendered meaningful what was once meaningless—all the waiting, all the raised-and-dashed hopes, all the patience and perseverance that characterized Sue's and my relationship for many years. I am not the author of my desires—this has become clear; I can only respond to them as they arise. This pilgrimage over the past sixteen years has taught me that in discerning where my desires come from, I learn how I might respond to them in ways that give us joy. And in the end, I have learned to attend to the whisperings of desire to find the places where God might be inviting me to grow, to change, and to stretch toward the freedom of the real me, the person who can share joy with the women he loves most.

Questions for Couples in Love

Chapter 1

Question 1, p. 2:   "Her certainty about this decision came long before mine, and often since the onset of her alternately forceful and gentle persuasions I have found myself facing this reality like a brick wall."

Have you ever found yourself to be at a much different place emotionally or mentally from that of your loved one? If so, did one or both of you recognize it at once, or did you discover this difference as time went on?

How have you dealt with the two of you not being in the same place at the same time?

Question 2, p. 4:   "Oh, nothing." I've learned that this is the answer I reach for when she's asked something I find hard to talk about. It's the shut-down-the-conversation-before-it's-begun answer, the I-find-it-difficult-to-admit-I'm-really-unnerved-by-this-whole-thing answer."

Have you noticed ways in which you or your loved one shut down difficult conversations? Are there also ways you've learned to open up the conversation? What are you learning about openness and resistance while trying to discuss important issues?

Chapter 2

Question 3, p. 15:   "I encounter beauty everywhere; in the many museums, cathedrals, and town squares I've found after perusing my *Let's Go Europe*, but I encounter it alone. I am constantly reminded of the presence of her absence."

When did you first realize that your life was not really full without the presence of the person you loved? What experiences helped you understand that your life should unfold with this person instead of without him/her?

Question 4, p. 26:   "That terrifying and exhilarating kiss stripped me of my defenses, my rationality, the facade of my persona, and all that was left was the barest reality of what was true deep within: I loved her, and she loved me."

Was there a pivotal point in your lives together that marked the transition from friendship to a romantic relationship? How did this specific action, whether a kiss or a discussion, set the tone for your new relationship?

Chapter 3

Question 5, p. 43:   "These couple of days will have to be simply a glance into my world, a short peek into what has become for me my whole life. What will she think when she sees it? Will she see a confident, brilliant young man. . . . Or will she see the truth, the real me, the one who is just flying at breakneck speed in the hope that moving fast will somehow get me to where I'm supposed to be?"

When you and your loved one were first getting to know each other, were there parts of yourself you were reluctant or even embarrassed to share? In the time since then, have you grown

more confident in his/her acceptance of you, or do you still fear that the "real" you won't be good enough?

Question 6, p. 49:   "She did not come from a wealthy family, and I knew that money was a sensitive subject. It was, I think, the thing that terrified me the most last spring when I had the inner turmoil over whether I could tell her that I loved her. What could I give her? What was I asking her to be part of? Transience, waiting until I finished my degrees, living on next-to-nothing?"

When you entered this relationship, what expectations did you have of yourself? What expectations did you imagine the other person had of you?

Chapter 4

Question 7, p. 56:   "The truth is that over the past months my friendship with one of the women here is starting to make me nervous. Amy is sweet and understands that I am attached; . . . She is a good person and would never seek to hurt anyone. But I know we are attracted to each other; our conversations are easy and engaging. We like spending time together, even though it has almost always been in a group."

Have you ever felt that another friendship might be threatening in some way to this relationship? If so, what were the signals? Did you see them right away, or did someone else point them out to you?

Other attractions can also threaten relationships. Have you ever felt that a pastime or interest became so important that it became a problem between the two of you?

Question 8, p. 59:   "It was a profound experience of prayer, of bringing what I was thinking and feeling into conversation with God and asking for a little clarity.... The idea of ending my relationship with Sue was so horrible ... In my physical training over the years I had experienced the satisfaction of sacrificing one thing in order to have another, and this decision about my relationships felt similar. I felt stronger and more resolved that I was doing the right thing, both for Sue and for me."

The prayer that Tim describes in this situation is actually a form of prayer found in Ignatian spirituality. When trying to discern between one option and another, the person pays close attention to interior movements, known as consolation and desolation. Tim experienced sadness when he imagined not pursuing a relationship with Amy. But he experienced a devastating loss when he imagined ending his relationship with Sue in order to pursue another relationship. In paying attention to his truest desires, he was able to make a clear-headed choice. This discernment process is useful for any sort of decision making because it honors the wisdom of the deep emotional life as well as the values a person has already chosen. For more on discernment, go to www.ignatianspirituality.com.

What factors have helped guide your decisions about relationships? Which factors were helpful, and which seemed more harmful?

Chapter 5

Questions 9, p. 65:   "At some point in those early months, we both recognized an important truth: waiting for stability before embarking on marriage was absurd. We were struggling against the assumption that we had to already have our financial and professional lives in order before we could marry; that assumption was one of the unwritten social codes that prevailed among so many of our peers. The implication, it seemed, was that one had to present to the future spouse a "package"—a marriage-ready partner, complete with plans for income, living arrangement, childbearing and raising, job- and chore-sharing, and so on. It was part of the unwritten contract for marriage."

What assumptions did you have about "being ready" to be married? Were you being idealistic, or realistic? What kinds of adjustments in thinking did you have to make before going through with the marriage?

Question 10, p. 69:   "'I will give you something you can be sure of,' I said, running to the other room. I retrieved the ring and the poem from my bag, went back to her, knelt down while looking into her tearstained face, and asked her to marry me."

Did your "proposal" work out according to plan, or did something else happen? Was there an official proposal, or did the two of you agree to marry in some other way? How did that agreement fit into what was going on in your lives at the time?

Chapter 6

Question 11, p. 77:   "I understood that there was a deep and abiding connection between the physical and the spiritual. It was hard to train when feeling depressed; it was exciting to train when riding a high. A great workout could produce feelings of elation, and a sluggish one could produce lethargy. Even over the

first three days we became attuned to the long-lingering consequences of sex, heightening our abilities to attend to the other in
the more mundane moments of the day. Did she need a foot rub?
Or a shoulder squeeze? Was her expression showing a feeling of
sadness or pain?"

**How have you experienced your sexual life together as con-
nected to the rest of life? How has sex changed the way you
communicate in other areas?**

Chapter 7

Question 12, p. 82:   "'So you're comfortable inviting people
over with a tablecloth over the window?' It was white, with red,
blue, and green flowers, arranged kind of like a curtain. Not bad,
I thought, until this moment."

**What are the differences between the two of you in terms of
priorities? How have you discovered those differences, and
what have you done to work them out?**

Question 13, p. 85:   "I was attracted to this new expression of
her personality; it made me happy to think about all the gifts
that she had. And it made me even happier to realize that this is
my wife. . . . "You were amazing," I said, somewhat blandly. "I've
never seen that side of you before."

**Has there been a time or an event that revealed to you a new
side of your loved one's personality? Describe what that was
like for you. How does it make you feel to know that this
person you love expresses various aspects of his/herself to
other people in various situations?**

Chapter 8

Question 14, p. 93: "I can't even remember how I shot down the suggestion. I felt punched in the stomach by the idea, which seemed so far off my radar screen that I didn't even know how to interpret my response to it. I wasn't yet at the point of believing that there was any problem to be solved, and she was offering what seemed to me a life-changing solution. Implicitly, and probably explicitly, I indicated that I was not on board with this idea."

Which one of you is the first to identify problems in your life together? When that problem is presented in conversation, how does the other person respond? Which of you is first to express fear, anxiety, or caution? Which of you is the first to start working on a solution? How does this affect your relationship in general?

Question 15, p. 96: "We have moved a long way from the sexual script that I remember in my early years in college. Today I am pulled in different directions: the desire to comfort her in her pain, the desire to cooperate with her in the process of diagnosis and prognosis; the desire to let her know that I will walk with her on this new phase of our pilgrimage, regardless of the still-unknown destination."

How has your sexual script changed during your relationship, and what has caused the change? Do you consider this change for the better or for the worse? Does it help each of you if you identify the change and its cause?

Chapter 9

Question 16, p. 99:   "It's becoming less and less likely that a pregnancy is in our future. We've seen specialists, we've tried the fertility drugs, but nothing is working. We've talked about the possibility of in vitro fertilization. But more and more we feel we are becoming subjected to a kind of reproductive technology machine that is playing on our desire to become parents. Neither of us wants to go down that road, in large part because we could never choose to selectively abort viable embryos."

Infertility gave Tim and Sue reason to cry out to God. In the lives of most couples, there is at least one issue that leads to some kind of desperation. What is that issue in your life together? Have you been able to translate frustration, anger, and desperation into prayers that cry out to God? If not, can you think of a way to begin such a prayer?

Question 17, p. 102:   "Søren Kierkegaard wrote of faith as a leap into an unknown; this was what I was feeling. It was love for her that moved me to this act of trust in her judgment, even though I felt scared and unsure of what to anticipate."

Have you ever taken a leap of faith to support your loved one? How did your love for this person reassure you even in times of uncertainty?

Chapter 10

Question 18, p. 110:   "My years of competitive rowing . . . were some of the best of my life. I felt alive, able to take on any struggle. I suppose that this year I wanted to recapture some of that. But at the same time it was nice to realize that I no longer cling to racing as the place where my life struggles play out. This race was more of a parable, similar to the many stories of hope that unfold at every Boston Marathon. Here are the people racing to raise money for cancer research; there are the people racing in memory of a loved one. . . . For me, the race was about moving beyond the years of defeat and hardship, heartbreak and hopelessness, and committing myself to looking forward to adoption. I had promised Sue more than two years ago that I would one day be ready, and that day has come."

At some point, we must shift to a new center in life. For Tim, it was a shift from life as a single man active in academia and competitive rowing to the life he had chosen with Sue. Has there been a definite shift for you, or has the adjustment happened gradually and not so noticeably?

Does this shift from life-before-marriage to life-after-marriage represent some losses to you? How have you processed the losses attached to life-before-marriage?

Question 19, p. 111: "Having a counseling background herself, Sue was wise enough to begin seeing a counselor before it became a crucial necessity. I stretched my capacity to comfort her in her pain but at the same time was coming to name and acknowledge my own. Sue recognized this and understood that she needed someone besides me to help her process the many emotions she had to withstand daily. I was relieved; although I was doing everything I could, before long I realized that I could help her only so much. I simply wasn't equipped emotionally to understand all that she was going through. It was one of those times when I had to face my limitations, even in this great love relationship. It hurt me too much to talk with her at great length about how much she was hurting."

Have both of you recognized your limitations when it comes to loving and caring for one another? Where do you find the help you cannot receive from your loved one? Where does he/she find help outside of your relationships?

Question 20, p. 113:   "We held on to that script—I more than she, perhaps because she is more in tune with the wisdom of her emotions. As the data of our lives made the script less and less relevant, I was left with the need to find another plotline. And when we finally had to toss out the script altogether, I discovered that she had been developing a perfectly good alternate all along."

What script did you have for love and marriage when you first started this journey? How has that script changed, and how have the two of you responded to that change?

Chapter 11

Question 21, p. 128:   "We have come a long, long way. The irony that the pilgrimage of our relationship has brought us to the other side of the earth—the longest possible journey—is not lost on either of us. It began as a desire to know one another, to be present to each other, to spend time discovering ourselves in conversation with the other. Our early relationship began as a seed of friendship, which germinated in attraction and flowered into a transcontinental romance. But that was only the first phase of this pilgrimage. . . . Recalling the spring of my sophomore year in college, when I stayed awake nights thinking about her, I can see that there was a deep heart-wisdom, a knowledge that my restless heart was reaching out to her as one whose presence would bring me peace. I have learned to trust that wisdom in light of the past few years, when ordinary left-brain thinking would have kept me from trusting Sue's intuitions."

Most people operate more out of their analytic thinking (left brain) or more out of their intuition (right brain)—which type of thinking does each of you tend to use most? Have your tendencies toward analysis or intuition caused friction between you? If so, how have you dealt with it? Have you noticed how your ways of approaching life might complement each other?

Chapter 12

Question 22, p. 132:   "Falling in love is dangerous and therefore thrilling, because it means that your happiness is irrevocably tied up in the life of another sovereign creature. It means that you relinquish any illusion of being capable of managing life, because its complications are multiplied by the very fact that you care deeply about everything that impinges on the lives of those you love. . . . The happy times may be multiplied, but so too the experiences of pain; there are simply more of both because of the number of travelers. Today I wish there was a bank in which we could save this experience, to draw upon it later, when I will say to them, "Remember what a beautiful day it was at Disneyland? And how we all felt so happy to be there together?" I will certainly remind them of this moment when they are having bad dreams or are unsure of whether the world can be a hospitable place."

Do you agree or disagree that it's dangerous to fall in love? What has love cost you, and what has it given you? How has your journey changed because of it?

ABOUT THE AUTHOR

Tim Muldoon is a theologian and author of several books, including *The Ignatian Workout* (Loyola Press). Currently, he teaches in the Honors Program at Boston College, where he also serves in the Office of University Mission and Ministry. He lives with his wife, two daughters, and mother-in-law in Natick, Massachusetts.